POLICE IN CANADA

POLICE IN CANADA

THE REAL STORY

JOHN SEWELL

LORIMER

JAMES LORIMER & COMPANY LTD., PUBLISHERS
TORONTO

James Lorimer & Company Ltd., Publishers acknowledges the support of the Ontario Arts Council. We acknowledge the financial support of the Government of Canada through the Canada Book Fund for our publishing activities. We acknowledge the support of the Canada Council for the Arts for our publishing program. We acknowledge the Government of Ontario through the Ontario Media Development Corporation's Ontario Book Initiative.

Cover design: Meghan Collins
Cover image: Istock

Library and Archives Canada Cataloguing in Publication

Sewell, John, 1940-
    Police in Canada : the real story / by John Sewell.

Includes bibliographical references and index.
Issued also in electronic format.
ISBN 978-1-55277-521-9

    1. Police--Canada. I. Title.

HV8157.S493 2010   363.20971   C2010-902606-3

James Lorimer & Company Ltd., Publishers
317 Adelaide Street West, Suite 1002
Toronto, ON, Canada
M5V 1P9
www.lorimer.ca

Printed in Canada

CONTENTS

PREFACE

MY INTEREST IN POLICING ISSUES BEGAN WHEN I WAS A MEMBER OF TORONTO City Council during the 1970s and early 1980s. When teaching at York University in the early 1980s, I was asked to devise a course on policing, and that led to my 1985 book, *Police: Urban Policing in Canada.*

As I turned to other activities my interest did not wane, but there was always a problem of finding a forum for expressing ideas about police. In the late 1990s, I helped establish the Toronto Police Accountability Coalition (TPAC). For more than a decade, this organization has met monthly to try to understand the policing world and to discuss police policies in a constructive manner. It hasn't always been easy. For instance, Toronto police chief Julian Fantino sued me for libel and slander for what he said was a misinterpretation of a Supreme Court of Canada ruling about the way the Toronto police force carried out strip searches. I had to find money to retain a lawyer and agree to apologize for what-ever I had said, but in that apology I stated that I would continue to press for a better strip-search policy to be used by Toronto police. (As noted in this book, we were not successful in reducing the number of strip searches carried out by Toronto police: almost one-third of all those arrested are strip searched, even though the Supreme Court stated that strip searching should be done rarely.) TPAC has produced a bimonthly electronic bulletin since 2002 (available at www.tpac.ca), and it traces many policing issues in Toronto over this eight-year period.

Then, in 2007, I taught a one-semester course in policing at Ryerson University. This book emerged as a result of that activity. In writing *Police in Canada*, I have been amazed at just how little has changed since 1985. Some of the most interesting thinking about police activities occurred in the 1970s and 1980s (as one notes from the essays in David Bayley's recent book, *What Works in Policing*), and since then it seems most police forces have been closed to experimentation and external study. This makes the case for needed change all that more urgent.

I thank my friend Jim Lorimer for asking me to do this book, and for the editorial assistance of Diane Young at Lorimer, and Alison Reid.

This book is dedicated to my long-term colleagues at TPAC, Anna, Richard, Harvey, and Else Marie, who have been strong friends in reviewing and acting on this most important of public policy issues over the years.

1

MAKING SENSE OF CRIME STATISTICS

THE WORD "CRIME" HAS AN OMINOUS RING TO IT. IT SUGGESTS UNPREDICTABLE violence that could affect any of us at any time. We assume that crime is everywhere around us, ready to strike if we let our guard down, or if the police do not form that thin blue line between us and imminent danger.

This is, of course, not an accurate or helpful way to look at crime in Canada. The rate of violent crime is in fact fewer than one thousand incidents a year for every hundred thousand Canadians. Most violent crime consists of assaults (such as fist fights) not serious enough to require hospital treatment. Violent crime involving more than simple assault is rare, and not many families have direct experience with it. The number of homicides in Canada, for instance, is fewer than six hundred a year, which for a population of more than 30 million is very low. Most homicides occur between persons known to each other, infrequently between strangers.

There are about 2.5 million criminal charges laid each year in Canada. About half are for property crimes, 300,000 are for crimes of violence, and the remainder are for assorted criminal activities. Generally, police officers lay three or four charges against each individual for a single criminal act, and the number of persons charged annually is in the order of 750,000. It is certain that some individuals are charged for a number of different incidents in a single year, so the number of persons charged with one or more criminal offences in Canada in a year is in the range of 600,000.

Perhaps a more helpful way of getting a handle on the number of crimes is to look at them in relation to the number of public police officers. Few of us understand how much crime the average police officer in a large city must deal with during a shift, or in a week. Such data are fairly uniform across the country: the average Canadian police officer can expect to make seven or eight criminal arrests a year, or one arrest every six or seven weeks. The majority of these crimes involve property, not violence to a person.

Another helpful comparison in estimating the impact of crime is statistics for violent deaths other than homicide. In Toronto, for instance, there are about sixty-five homicides every year, but seventy-five people are killed, and a further twenty-three thousand are injured, in car accidents. The risk of death or injury related to automobiles is much higher than the same risk related to a crime. Another example: Canadians greatly fear child abductions. These frightening events are relatively rare, and their number pales in comparison with that of children killed each year in automobile accidents. A 2003 study by the Royal Canadian Mounted Police found that 5 children were abducted by strangers in the years 2001 to 2002; the number of children killed in traffic accidents in the years 2000 to 2001 (not quite the same two-year period) was 282, and a further 21,827 children were injured. Thus, the fear of violent injury or death should be directed more to the automobile than to crime.

In Canada there are about seventy violent deaths each year for every hundred thousand people. The breakdown of those deaths is revealing: traffic accidents, eighteen; other accidents, thirty-six; suicide, thirteen; homicide, two. Crime carries a powerful imaginative weight in Western society, but as this evidence shows, the fear it invokes far surpasses the reality of its small incidence.

Crime rates between countries differ. Annual comparisons between Canada and the United States for every hundred thousand people are as follows:

	Canada	United States
Homicide	2	5.5
Serious assault	143	324
Robbery	88	145
Break and enter	954	724
Car theft	521	414

What may be more interesting is that the incidence of crime is not uniform across Canada but varies from city to city and from province to province. Annual crime rates are highest in Saskatchewan, almost seven thousand criminal offences per hundred thousand population, compared with Quebec and Ontario, where the rate is in the order of twenty-one hundred. Manitoba has a rate of fifty-one hundred, Alberta about four thousand, British Columbia forty-five hundred. It is not entirely clear why these rates differ; they undoubtedly relate to slight variations in culture in the various parts of the country, and may reflect the Go West attitude: people who experience problems in the eastern parts of North America have for more than a century gone west to seek their fortune, with, in some cases, unanticipated results.

It's also fascinating that annual crime rates are generally higher in small urban areas—that is, communities which are not one of the twenty-seven census metropolitan areas as defined by Statistics Canada—than in large urban ones: there are about seven thousand Criminal Code offences for every hundred thousand residents of large cities compared with just over ten thousand for residents of small cities. Crime rates in rural areas are in the order of sixty-five hundred per hundred thousand. The rate of violent crime in small urban areas is 1200 for every 100,000 residents, whereas in large cities it is 830. That relationship does not hold for homicide rates, which are slightly higher in large cities, nor for robbery, which is twice as high in big cities and nine times higher than in rural areas. Motor vehicle theft occurs much more frequently in large urban centres than in other places. Opportunity probably accounts for higher rates of robbery and car theft in large cities, but trying to account for the general differences in these crime rates is not easy because of unpredictable or contradictory factors. Some data, for example, indicate that city residents take precautionary measures such as regularly locking their cars or staying on the alert, perhaps unlike inhabitants of other places in the country. Obviously in large cities there are more "eyes on the street" and thus more neighbourhood support, which could result in lower crime rates. However, as a general point, crime rates are higher in smaller centres, and those who choose to live there because they are "safer" have certainly not made that decision based on familiarity with crime rates.

Statistics Canada, working with police officials, has recently adopted a "crime severity" index, which gives more weight to serious crimes and less weight to those crimes such as mischief and minor theft, since the latter group are not seen as a real threat to public safety. (The index does not include traffic or drug crimes.) The index shows serious crime for various cities as follows: Regina 189; Saskatoon 158; Winnipeg 153; Abbotsford 142; Edmonton 131; Vancouver 128; Thunder Bay 115; Victoria 106; Halifax 106; St. John's 100. The remaining cities with a population of more than one hundred thousand all have indices of under 100. Montreal, Calgary and London are in the 90s; Hamilton, Windsor, Gatineau and St. Catharines are in the 80s; Ottawa, Sudbury, Sherbrooke and Kingston are in the 70s; and Quebec City and Toronto are in the 60s.

These indices reveal very significant variations. The severe crime rate in Regina is twice what it is in Calgary, three times what it is in Toronto; Edmonton's is twice Quebec City's.

How can these large differences be explained? Some think that the high percentage of aboriginal persons in some cities skews the serious crime rates, but is that mostly because they are arrested more often than other Canadians (and their rate of incarceration is far higher than other Canadians)? If aboriginal citizens were deemed disproportionately responsible for crime, that could imply either significant racial profiling by police and/or a criminal culture in the aboriginal community. There is no strong evidence for the latter. No one has credibly made the argument that the differences result from policing techniques or the number of police officers per capita, probably because it cannot be sustained. Without viable explanations for the differences, creating an agenda for reducing crimes rates in those cities is not easy.

Most crime—more than 80 per cent—is caused by males under the age of thirty; evidence from many Western countries indicates that violent crime rates peak among males in their late teens to early twenties. Less than 20 per cent of crime is caused by females, though female rates of crime are higher with respect to shoplifting and writing bad cheques. It is unclear how to account for the dramatic distinction between male and female crime rates. Do females have fewer opportunities for crime? Are they more socially minded? Is biology a factor, perhaps something related to the presence or absence of testosterone? It is probably reasonable to say that no one explanation exists.

And there are inherent problems with crime statistics themselves: not all crime is reported to the police. What remains unreported has been called the "dark figure of crime," and it is significant. Murders are sometimes hidden by families, disguised as accidents, or treated as disappearances. For instance, the disappearances of many young Canadian women (often active in the sex trade) have frequently been shrugged off by police, perhaps because of the perceived low social status of the victims, until the number of similar incidents becomes so large that the public and then the police see a recognizable pattern and suspect murder. This sequence occurred in several parts of the country. In the Vancouver area in 2002, Robert Pickton was charged with twenty-six counts of first-degree murder involving women from the city's Downtown Eastside over a period of more than ten years. Also in British Columbia, along the "Highway of Tears," more than a dozen young aboriginal women have vanished in the past decade. In Winnipeg in 2009, police and provincial officials began an investigation when it was alleged that more than 30 women had disappeared over a period of several decades, though activists say that about 160 women are missing and presumed murdered. Similar stories about women's disappearances have been heard in Edmonton, Regina, and Saskatoon. It is generally thought that for every murder known to authorities, three or four are not reported or not treated as homicide.

Many sexual crimes such as rape and indecent assault also go unreported for the obvious reason that the women attacked fear the consequences of complaining and/or presume they will not be believed. The understanding is that only one of every ten rapes or indecent assaults are actually reported. Similarly, many thefts go unreported because they are regarded as too minor to involve authorities or because the aggrieved person doesn't feel the incident is worth the time and trouble to pursue officially. Many frauds go unreported because the aggrieved person might look foolish for having been taken in.

There are, in fact, a number of reasons why people don't report crimes they know about: they may believe police won't take effective action, that the offender may not be identified or caught, that reporting and following through could take too much of their time, that there may be retaliation; or they may have been personally involved (for instance, receiving stolen goods). In some cases, a crime is not reported because a private settlement is worked out between the parties.

The incidence of the dark figure of crime varies, but in general it is substantial, and probably no more than one-third to one-half of all criminal events are actually reported to the police.

The late Richard V. Ericson, an author and the director of the Centre of Criminology, University of Toronto, quarreled with the whole notion of "the dark figure of crime" and states,

> *To ask 'how big is the dark figure?' is to pose a question of the same logical order as 'how long is a piece of string?' or 'how many grains of wheat are there in a heap?' For all practical purposes, crime only consists of those acts that are so designated by the police for their crime control purposes on behalf of the authorities. The necessary condition for crime is the police designation ... In this formulation, it is meaningless to use the concept of a 'dark figure' of crime. We can study the process by which the police discover things which they make into crimes and how they do organizational bookkeeping to keep count of crimes, but we shall never know the total volume of things out there that could be made into crimes.*

Perhaps this definition of crime is academic: many events exhibit widely recognized characteristics of crime even if the police don't lay charges. At the same time, there are circumstances in which the police decide for good reason not to lay charges, or instead to give a warning. They may decide in a tense public situation to overlook certain actions that, if arrests were made, would cause considerable disorder, such as at a demonstration. They may decide a particular problem is unresolvable and that the possibility of identifying someone who could be charged is very small. There may be an unwritten rule that certain events don't result in police action (such as cars travelling at 120 km/h in a 100 km/h zone.) Or the police may have social prejudices shared by the larger society that lead them not to lay charges, as in the disappearances of the young women already discussed.

There are allegations that police lay charges when they shouldn't. The possession of marijuana is one such instance that has led to contention, and some have argued that though the law is clear, the police should show discretion for the possession of small amounts of the drug. It is known that in British Columbia, where there is a very large market for growing and selling marijuana, police rarely lay charges for possession, and this response seems generally supported by the public. In Ontario in 2009 one newspaper report claimed that criminal justice courts were overloaded because the police laid too many minor charges that should have been merely warnings. The question of when the police lay charges requires a full discussion of police discretion and will be addressed in a later chapter.

Despite what seems to be a rising worry about crime, since the mid-1990s the crime rate in Canada—and in the United States—has been falling. In 1983 the American political scientist James Q. Wilson predicted that the drop would take place. He wrote, "By 1990 about half a million fewer eighteen-year-old males will be living in this country [United States] than were living here in 1979. As everyone knows young males commit proportionately more crimes than older ones. Since it is the case in general that about 6 percent of young males become chronic offenders; if each chronic offender commits 10 offenses (a conservative estimate) per year, we will have a third of a million fewer crimes from this age group alone." His prediction has come true, and the demographic mix shows fewer young males, which might account for some of the change.

There may be other factors; finding reasons for changes in crime rates is not easy. In his 2003 book, *Why Crime Rates Fell*, John Conklin, a professor of sociology at Tufts University in Massachusetts, looks at the precipitous decline in rates of serious crime in the United States between 1990 and 1999. Murder rates fell 39 per cent, robberies 42 per cent, burglary 36 per cent, motor vehicle theft 36 per cent. (General crime rates have fallen about 30 per cent across Canada during the past two decades.) Drops were evident in New York City too, and Conklin tried to determine causes there, quickly dismissing the claim of New York City police that they had done something special, since the declines were countrywide. He concludes that the decline is "not due to a decrease in reporting of crime to police," nor could it be explained by a natural cycle of some kind. He believes that "more effective gun control meas-ures reduced murder, more intensive police patrols cut robberies, more use of dead-bolt locks curbed burglaries, and more installation of car alarm systems decreased motor vehicle thefts." He writes that there are no data to indicate that the per capita size of the city's police force affects the crime rate, nor do the frequency of patrol cars or foot patrols, nor indeed community policing. He thinks that the stricter incarceration policies used in United States helped reduce crime since those released from jail often commit a dozen crimes a year, and if they are kept in jail without parole those crimes will not be committed.

Conklin believes that the decreased use of crack cocaine beginning in the late 1980s resulted in a reduction in crime because previous users were not committing criminal acts for the money needed to support their habit. He thinks that the shrinkage in the number of young males also had a positive minimal effect. Conklin maintains as well that the era's productive economy had some impact on dropping crime rates since economic security contributes to a stronger family unit, which in turn leads to less crime. Tellingly, among the factors that he concludes played roles in crime reduction, the activities of police seem to have had little impact.

Sometimes changes in crimes rates may be related to changes in law. In Canada in 1991, 1,444 people were killed with guns; in 1995, there were 1,125 such deaths, and by 2005 the number had fallen to 818. The best explanation for this large decrease is the 1995 introduction of the Canadian Firearms Registry requiring that long guns—shotguns and rifles—be registered as well as handguns. Homicides from rifles and shotguns have decreased almost by half from 1995 (61) to 2007 (32). There are, of course, those who object strongly to registering long guns, and politicians from all parties have urged that the registry's require-ments be loosened, but with such positive results, the law would appear to be very effective.

Convincing evidence exists that rates of crime in any country are related to its social equality—ideally, a circumstance affording all society's members the same legal status, essential rights, opportunities, security, and responsibilities. In *The Spirit Level: Why Greater Equality Makes Societies Stronger*, published in 2009, two English authors, Richard Wilkinson and Kate Pickett, bring together powerful material to indicate that the general well-being of any country can be measured by the degree of the income equality of its citizens, and the more signs there are of equality the better the welfare and functioning of that society will be. Similarly, the lower the equality, the worse the welfare and the lower the overall functioning.

The data they present in respect to violent criminal activity are also persuasive. The more economically unequal the residents of a country, the more common are homicides. In countries such as Japan, Norway, and Denmark, where there is considerable social equality and the gap between those at the bottom of society and those at the top is not vast, homicide rates are quite low. In countries where inequality is greater, such as the United States, homicide rates are very high. Canada is midpoint between the examples, reflected in its homicide rate, also at a midpoint—slightly higher than in Germany and the Netherlands, slightly lower than in France and Italy.

More revealing are data from various American states found in *The Spirit Level*. The more unequal a state's social situation, the more common are homicides. Accordingly, rates of homicide are low in New Hampshire, Utah, and Vermont, where social equality is highest; and homicide rates are highest in Louisiana, Mississippi, Alabama, and New Mexico, where social equality is lowest. The authors note that "increased inequality ups the stakes in the competition for status: status matters even more ... triggers to violence have involved threats—or perceived threats—to pride, acts that instigated feelings of humiliation or shame ... Violence is most often a response to disrespect, humiliation, and loss of face, and is usually a male response to these triggers."

Wilkinson and Pickett explain the difference in crime rates over the years in the United States as a function of changes to social equality. As already noted, crime began rising in the 1960s until it peaked in 1990 and slid until the early 2000s. The authors claim that during the 1990s there was an overall decline in inequality. "From the early 1990s in America there was a particularly dramatic decline in relative poverty and unemployment for young people at the bottom of the social hierarchy," concluding that "the association between inequality and violence is strong and consistent; it's been demonstrated in many different time periods and settings."

The authors also remark that those who are charged with crimes are more likely to have grown up in homes without a father present. They state, "60% of America's rapists, 72% of juvenile murderers, and 70% of long term prisoners grew up in fatherless homes," arguing that males in fatherless environments become even more concerned about status and thus even more prone to the triggers of threats to pride.

The general conclusion to be drawn from this discussion is that the best explanations for changes in rates of crime relate to social and economic trends. Those who would argue that more police activity or more police officers can result in reduced rates of crime have a difficult time finding supporting evidence for that conclusion. This conclusion is important when addressing directions that police might pursue or that society might take to produce less crime.

Since many assume that the end result of criminal activity is often jail, it makes sense to take a brief look at prison statistics. In Canada in 2007 about 270,000 individuals were incarcerated in jail; some 90,000 had been convicted and sentenced to a jail term; just over 150,000 were in jail on remand awaiting trial; and a further 30,000 were in jail for other reasons, such as awaiting sentence. It is quite extraordinary that more than half the people in jail had never been convicted of a crime but were awaiting trial. The law in Canada is that when charged with a crime, you will be released on bail providing the judge is convinced that you will attend your trial and that you will not reoffend in the interim. The high number of people in jail awaiting a trial is a result of the significant degree of homelessness in Canada. Judges fear releasing individuals who do not have a permanent home but live on the street or in a shelter. They are often remanded into prison because there is no defined place where they can be located in case they do not attend their trial. In many cases these individuals face charges for relatively minor offences. Many suffer from mental illness of one kind or another, others suffer from addictions, and their personal demons result in activities that lead them to be charged and jailed. Jail is the most expensive way of dealing with them: in 2009 the cost of keeping a person in prison for one day was $170, whereas the cost of renting a small apartment was $30 a day, with support services probably costing the same amount. It would be much less expensive for society generally to provide housing and support services for these individuals; however, no government in Canada has moved definitively to reduce costs and reduce the rate of incarceration by providing housing and support services for those many persons on remand in jail.

Rates of incarceration have grown in recent years. In 2003 fewer than 70,000 persons were in jail after being convicted and sentenced; and fewer than 115,000 were on remand. There are three reasons for increasing imprisonment: a higher number of crimes committed; a greater tendency to send individuals to prison rather than trying other options; and longer sentences becoming usual. All three trends are apparent in Canada, resulting in more imprisonment and sometimes prison overcrowding.

In the United States, 12 per cent of the growth of the prison population in the past decade was the result of a rise in criminal offending, mostly because of drug activity; more important, judges were required by new laws to provide longer sentences. Legislation such as "three strikes," requiring a prison term for anyone convinced of three crimes, no matter how minor, has become more popular. Judges have also been stripped of their discretion (to make the punishment fit the crime) by new minimum mandatory sentences for many crimes. Programs have also been put in place to discourage early parole. In California in 2004, 360 individuals were serving life sentences for the crime of shoplifting. These trends have not been as noticeable in Canada but nevertheless do exist, as federal politicians try to argue that they want to be seen as tough on crime.

Most prisoners in Canada are male; in 2007 only 12 per cent were female. Aboriginals are substantially overrepresented in the prison population, comprising a staggering 25 per cent of all those in jail, even though they represent less than 3 per cent of the population of Canada.

Judges can decide on dispositions other than jail when sentencing, such as probation, conditional sentence, or conditional release. In 2007 there were 110,000 individuals who received such sentences: 83,000 were released on probation, 17,000 on conditional sentence (that is, a sentence that would be served in jail if they reoffended during a certain period of time), and 10,000 on conditional release (that is, they would be brought back to court if they reoffended).

The evidence provided by the authors of *The Spirit Level* shows that the more social inequality in a country, the greater its rate of imprisonment. Thus in Japan, Norway, Finland, and Sweden, imprisonment rates are very low. In the United States, imprisonment rates are very high. And, reflecting rates of homicide, the more social inequality there is in an American state the higher its imprisonment rate. The authors conclude that "more unequal societies are more punitive." They also note that "people of lower class, income, education are much more likely to be sent to prison than people higher up the social scale." Most of us know this from personal experience. Few middle-class individuals end up in jail.

Jails have a negative influence on behaviour, and rates of recidivism—relapsing into crime—are high. Jail is not a place where rehabilitation occurs with any great regularity; it seems to be a place where people learn how to commit more crimes. As some critics have noted, the most

21

effective way to turn a non-violent person into a violent one is to send him to jail. About two-thirds of all those who are sent to jail in the United States and the United Kingdom re-offend; in Sweden it is slightly more than one-third. In countries with greater social inequality, prisoners are often treated with little respect. One sheriff in Arizona, Joe Arpaio, has been noted for his extraordinarily punitive activities, including forcing prisoners to live in tents in the desert even though the temperature rises above forty degrees Celsius, and feeding them minimal food at a cost of less than twenty cents per person per meal. Given the low status of prisoners in Arizona, Arpaio is often praised by community leaders, even though the number of prisoners who have died while under his control is very high.

Apparently, putting more people in jail for longer periods of time will not help make us a safer society. Apparently, hiring more police officers will not help to reduce crime. It seems that creating a safer society with less crime has much more to do with broad social policy. It is in this context that police activities and structures are best reviewed.

2

POLICE WORK AND PRIVATE POLICING

THIS CHAPTER DEALS WITH THE WORK THAT POLICE FORCES DO, THE WORK OF private police, and the relationship between them.

Police duties are defined in legislation, and Section 42(1) of the *Police Services Act* in Ontario is representative of what is contained in legislation across Canada. The section states:

The duties of a police officer include,

(a) preserving the peace;

(b) preventing crimes and other offences and providing assistance and encouragement to other persons in their prevention;

(c) assisting victims of crime;

(d) apprehending criminals and other offenders and others who may lawfully be taken into custody;

(e) laying charges and participating in prosecutions;

(f) executing warrants that are to be executed by police officers and performing related duties;

(g) performing the lawful duties that the chief of police assigns;

(h) in the case of a municipal police force and in the case of an agreement under section 10 (agreement for provision of police services by the Ontario Provincial Police), enforcing municipal by-laws;

(i) completing the prescribed training.

This list describes the work of an officer almost entirely in terms of crime. It fits well with the portrayal of police as crime fighters in movies and television programs. Yet, the best estimates are that police spend only 15 per cent of their time dealing with criminal issues, and as already noted, the average officer makes no more than seven or eight arrests in a year. We all have some idea of the other things a police officer does—dealing with traffic issues, including malfunctioning traffic lights; providing order at parades and other public events; assisting people who can't look after themselves because of illness, addiction, or other causes of distress; responding to calls for service—but these are apparently not official duties.

Section 4 of the same *Act* is not much different. It outlines that every municipality in Ontario must provide police services, and states, "Adequate and effective police services must include, at a minimum … [c]rime prevention, law enforcement, assistance to victims of crime, public order maintenance, [and] emergency response." The major difference is the inclusion of "emergency response." Alberta's *Police Act* covers the same kinds of functions, with the addition that they "encourage and foster a co-operative relationship" between police and the community. Statutes in British Columbia, Saskatchewan, and Manitoba do not outline the duties of an officer.

Police also have much more power than others in the use of force. Section 25 of the Criminal Code states that an officer may use "as much force as necessary" in carrying out the law, though force causing death or serious injury can be used only to protect against death or serious injury. Police often cite this as the rationale for an action: they feared the other person would kill them, their partner, or another person.

One critical question is when and how an officer should enforce the law. Officers have considerable flexibility in how they will act, and a variety of actions can be taken in any situation. Take the classic instance of an officer stopping someone on the street. The officer can ask questions, frisk the person, tell the person to leave the area, arrest the person, threaten to use force, put handcuffs on the person, call more officers, and so forth. What should the officer do? The answer relates not just to the specifics of the incident, but also to what the officer perceives as the main task at hand. One set of actions may follow from the officer's decision that his or her key role in this instance is to keep the peace, another if he or she thinks the emphasis should be enforcing the law. And what the officer actually does is often a result of the actions of the person stopped. Most often the officer will ask for the consent of a person to do something for which the officer has no legal authority—such as searching a bag without a warrant—but the person knows that objecting to that search will lead to further trouble, and so consents. The powers of an officer expand enormously because of consent given under duress.

What should an officer do if you are jaywalking when there is no traffic? Ignore you? Give you a ticket? What should happen if you are driving on a major highway at 110 km/h or 120 km/h with a speed limit of 100 km/h? If you're smoking a joint at a rock concert? If you are bathing naked on a beach where others do the same? If you are tipsy coming out of a bar with your friends? Regardless of what the law says, should there be some public expectations about what the police response will be in a community?

These questions all involve what is known as police discretion. Some actions—indeed, virtually all options—involve selective enforcement of the law. There is no reason to believe that is a bad thing, since there is always a tension between keeping the peace and enforcing the law. And the need for discretion becomes even more apparent if one recognizes that the police do many kinds of work in addition to keeping the peace and enforcing the law. As well, there are other sorts of discretion, decisions are made at an organizational level rather than by an individual officer. Should a dispatcher decide to respond to a call by sending a patrol car? Should a foot patrol be assigned to an area? Do officers on horseback charge at demonstrators or wait them out? Should a deal be offered to a participant in a major crime when information is provided in exchange for reduced charges? Should officers be given tasers to subdue someone in a mental crisis, or should the police force invest in techniques to de-escalate crisis situations and calm suspects, perhaps by working with mental-health nurses?

There are many choices to be made in the way police work is done. Sometimes a general policy determines the boundaries of the exercise of discretion. For instance, a number of police forces have a policy that when police respond to a domestic dispute, one party, usually the man, will be charged. Is this reasonable? Occasionally the rule of "zero tolerance" is applied, with the assumption that police will lay charges for the smallest breach of the law (such as breaking a speed limit). Can instances of discretion be reduced to general rules? Or is the job of the police more complicated? Is it a matter of treating everyone essentially the same (for instance, no one driving at 110 km/h on a major highway will be charged unless there is some other problem) and also treating people fairly?

K.C. Davis in his 1969 book *Discretionary Justice* suggests a five-stage process in reaching discretionary decisions. First, admit that police don't enforce the law in every instance. Second, agree that selective enforcement is a good thing and should be open for all to debate and comment on. Third, senior officers should assist in setting principles on the way discretion is exercised. Fourth, the principles should be widely discussed and agreed on. Fifth, police should follow the results. The five stages seem to describe a reasonable approach to helping officers set limits on how they exercise their discretion, but unfortunately there is no police force that acknowledges using this method. The point is that stating that the function of a police officer is to lay charges and prevent crimes isn't helpful. It misses the key questions.

The American criminologist Herman Goldstein has suggested a different approach, one that makes a realistic assessment of police work and public expectations. His list of police duties includes the following:

1. To prevent and control conduct widely recognized as threatening to life and property (serious crime).
2. To aid individuals who are in danger of physical harm, such as the victim of a criminal attack or collision.
3. To protect constitutional guarantees such as the right of free speech and assembly.
4. To facilitate the movement of people and vehicles.
5. To assist those who cannot care for themselves, the intoxicated, the addicted, the mentally ill, the physically disabled, the old and the young.
6. To resolve conflict, whether it be between individuals, groups of individuals, or individuals and their government.
7. To identify problems which have the potential for becoming more serious problems for the individual citizen, for the police, and for the community (crime prevention).
8. To create and maintain a feeling of security in the community.

The list represents the panoply of police activities in the real world of North America, even if one duty may conflict with another (constitutional guarantees set against resolving conflict, for instance). But the importance of Goldstein's list is that unlike the legislated list of duties, it begins to define the skills that an officer will need, and it hints at the kinds of individuals needed for good police work. If the job of an officer is all about crime, the job will attract a certain kind of person. If it is about a number of things including crime, the job will attract other kinds of people. Getting the job description right is essential to having the job filled by an appropriate person.

Furthermore, the two job descriptions require different training and different management. This matter very significantly affects the way police work is structured. Unfortunately, the narrow definition of police work seems to be the one that is widely adopted, which means that many officers are badly equipped to do the work they are called on to do, and the management they work under is not well equipped to provide the style of leadership needed. Both of these subjects are discussed in later chapters.

What is clear is that the public police do not have a monopoly on activities related to safety and security. Public police play an important role, but others do as well. For instance, there are many organizations that act to prevent and control conduct widely recognized as threatening to life and property—that is, conduct denoted as serious crime—and the range of approaches they take to accomplish this goal is very wide. The gun control lobby takes a political approach, lobbying legislators for laws that will help keep guns out of the hands of those who could misuse them (and, looking at the gun deaths in Canada, one would have to conclude they are successful in their efforts). Children's Aid workers take actions to protect children. Private security guards are hired to control worrisome conduct, mostly in places that are not entirely public in nature. Mothers Against Drunk Driving is active in pushing for RIDE programs and tougher penalties for drunk drivers to ensure that drinking and driving is strongly sanctioned and sober drivers are protected. Security Commissions that monitor trading in stocks, bonds, and other financial instruments attempt to control criminal activities involving money. Schoolteachers and transit drivers play important but perhaps more passive roles in ensuring safety and security. Many groups, such as St. John's Ambulance or municipal emergency services, aid people hurt or in danger. Privately operated rape crisis centres play a most important role for women who have been attacked and need support. The Salvation Army has achieved an enviable reputation assisting the intoxicated, the addicted, the mentally ill, the physically disabled, the old and the young. Many social agencies, public and private, including the United

Way and the agencies it helps fund, are active in these areas—perhaps more effectively than the police, who may sometimes appear to shun troubled persons. Religious leaders work to resolve conflict, as do agencies offering mediation services. The urbanist Jane Jacobs noted that the feel of a city neighbourhood—its mix of uses, its density, its street design—is central to ensuring the presence of "eyes on the street" that prevent crime, and she maintained that active community organizations are the most effective tool for crime prevention. Data show that good social programs, particularly those directed at young mothers and their children, are far and away the most important tools for preventing crime. (Indeed, an argument can be made that the public police are almost impotent at preventing crime, much as their task is described with that objective.) Facilitating the movement of people and vehicles is done by police mostly in emergencies, abetted by citizens acting in a public-spirited manner, as they will in a crisis. Smart traffic planners design roads and sidewalks to minimize collisions. This partial list of examples of contributors to the prevention of serious crime, the protection against physical harm, and the provision of civic support services makes the point that the police are not alone in their functions.

Although public police are obligated to protect constitutional guarantees such as the right of free speech and assembly, they are not often seen as the essential organization offering these protections. Instead, one thinks of groups such as the Canadian Civil Liberties Association, the Law Union of Ontario, Pivot Legal Services in British Columbia, and some lawyers and judges. Often courageous elected politicians take on this role, even complaining that the police have not acted appropriately to permit free speech.

And is it the public police who create and maintain security in the community? Police forces claim this is a key function, but whether they can deliver is open to question. Clifford Shearing, director of the Centre of Criminology, Faculty of Law, University of Cape Town, argues that security is not a thing but a state of mind. We all certainly want it, but it is intangible. Some people believe that only police can provide security, so if you feel insecure, you should hire more police—not exactly the answer. What a police officer can offer is the threat of force. Yet that rarely creates more of a sense of security, just as carrying handguns is not likely to make us feel any safer.

In fact, security comes from a variety of sources in response to assorted potential threats. Security can come from knowing city hall has building inspectors on staff; from the licensing of cab drivers; from bars being held responsible for patrons who drink too much; from some curfews; from well-functioning community centres; from laws controlling guns; from responsible landlords and shop owners; from private security guards; from school crossing guards; from reliable banks; and from some community activists. Security comes in a number of forms: symbolic, cultural, political, social, and economic. A sense of security comes from a network of forces and situations working independently but supporting one another. It is incorrect to assume that police have a monopoly on security. The police force is a powerful and very well funded organization, often portrayed as the only important one concerned with our security, but any rational person would find the world an insecure and unsafe place if there were only a public police force to rely on.

This observation has not gone unnoticed, which is why private companies provide private policing, whether for themselves or for others. In 2008 there were just over one hundred thousand people employed by private security firms in Canada, compared with slightly more than sixty thousand public police officers.

Policing began as a private activity, when companies hired private guards to protect shipping on the Thames River in London in the late eighteenth century. It was so successful that it was made into a public function, and combined with the initiative of the Bow Street runners who were hired to catch criminals or to prevent crime by watching and undertaking patrols, it finally morphed into the police system established in England by Robert Peel in 1829. Even with public police forces, some firms continued to retain their own private forces, whether because they wanted a show of authority they could control themselves, or because of a sense that public police would not provide adequate security. Thus, in the United States, the Rockefellers hired the Pinkerton company to control Colorado strikers in the early twentieth century. Wackenhut is another American company available for corporate work. More recently, the Bush administration hired Blackwater to provide a private army twenty-five thousand strong in Iraq.

Three reasons are often given for the growth in the number of private security officers. First, some companies have become very large and require an internal mechanism to increase corporate security and protect their large factories and property holdings. Before declaring bankruptcy in 2009, General Motors controlled the fifth-largest police force in the United States. Also, as already noted, companies that control their own police force have more say over how that force operates than they could ever expect from public police.

Second, the nature of property has changed. Many large companies, particularly those in retail and entertainment, have vast property holdings onto which they invite the public. Such property—a shopping mall, an airline terminal, a public housing project, an apartment block, or a football field—has been referred to as "mass private property." There are restrictions on what public police officers may do on private property, even if it is readily open to the public: they can enter to prevent a crime from occurring, or they can enter to arrest someone fleeing, but in other cases, unless invited, they cannot enter unless they have obtained a search warrant. Given these limitations, companies find it easier to employ their own security officers to keep order, prevent crime, and generally provide security to those using mass private property. Usually security personnel are uniformed, but sometimes they are not. Staff who stand by the front door at retail enterprises to greet customers as they enter are largely playing a policing role, both letting shoppers know that they are being watched and being on hand to confront anyone who seems to be stealing goods.

Third, some organizations feel that they have difficulty getting public police to respond to their concerns or that the police have their own agenda. Thus, merchants on retail strips in many Canadian cities hire private security guards to provide general surveillance, even though it is often assumed that public police provide this service. Some municipalities, believing public police cannot do the job, have retained private security firms to provide policing services in parks.

The powers of private police and security officers are limited, though these powers are often expanded with the consent of those involved, a consent often freely given since it is one of the costs of admission onto the property. Of course private security can arrest anyone committing an offence on the property, but that differs little from the power available to any member of the public—anyone can arrest another person committing an offence. Private security officers do not have the ability to use force. Private security can search bags or clothing only with consent, but since entry to the property is often denied if the search is denied, consent is freely given. The best example of intrusive search occurs at airports, but without agreeing to that search, a traveller will not get on an airplane. The use of a uniform immediately imbues the security officer with power, just as the request to answer a few questions is usually met with answers when it is obvious that the security officer can threaten to call the public police.

One of the most significant powers of the private security officer, particularly in a shopping mall, is to issue a trespass notice stating that management deems the presence of the named individual undesirable, and that the individual will be arrested and prosecuted under the *Trespass to Property Act* if found on the property in the future. Guards use this means to keep undesirables off the property, and they determine, without a hearing or a trial, who they think are undesirable. Often those deemed undesirable are the homeless or youth, but the category can also include those who would dare to hold up a protest sign. Trespass notices are thought to be issued by mall owners with great regularity.

There are three important distinctions between public and private police. Private policing directs most of its energy at crime prevention, including close surveillance, controlling access to certain areas by denying entry to anyone without the appropriate identity card, and so forth. Public policing is much more concerned with apprehension after a crime has been committed, though random patrol is apparently undertaken in the expectation it will prevent crime (though, as pointed out later, this expectation is in reality not borne out).

Second, public police are concerned with blame, retribution, and punishment. Private policing does not share those concerns, opting instead for control that often seems swift and arbitrary (such as banning certain individuals from a mall). Occasionally the controlling actions cross reasonable lines, as was the case when one Canadian university denied degrees to students with outstanding traffic tickets.

Third, there are few legal constraints on the private police officer, and few rights available to the public, though this situation is beginning to change. In 2008 Ontario brought in the *Private Security and Investigative Services Act*, requiring private security officers who protect property or people (the word *protect* in the context seems vague) to obtain a licence and keep it in good standing. Security officers must be at least eighteen years of age, eligible to work in Canada, and without a serious criminal record. The legislation establishes that training is required, and also sets a code of conduct that includes a duty to be respectful, to show no discrimination, and to use no drugs or alcohol.

Special constables are halfway between public and private police officers. They are most often employed by semi-public bodies such as transit authorities, universities, or public housing authorities in order to police the mass private property of these bodies. Their appointment is often confirmed by the local policing authority, and though they do not have the same training as public police officers, they are given powers of arrest and often act like private security in issuing trespass notices.

Since they are policing what to all intents and purposes is space for a public service, they seem to provoke more complaints than other private security.

Should there be concern that private policing represents the privatization of a public service? Given the expansion in the number of public officers, and the large expenditures on public officers, this concern is rarely heard. Moreover, there is only occasional worry that their operations enjoin civil liberties, perhaps because their powers are so limited. Some observers, like Clifford Shearing, take the view that the rise of private policing is useful because it provides an alternative to public police, and in any case the focus should be on the policing done, not whether it is publicly or privately done. He believes that policing should be located primarily in the institutions of civil society rather than in the state, since the former arrangement better serves the complicated nature of civil society and its many different kinds of community. He maintains that the public police should have their role defined as solvers of specific kinds of problems (particularly involving the use of force) rather than as all-purpose problem solvers. David H. Bayley, dean of the School of Criminal Justice, State University of New York, Albany, makes similar arguments in *Police for the Future.*

There are few formal links between public and private police, and descriptions of how the two policing models work in places such as Vancouver, Halifax, and Edmonton suggest that they are sometimes at cross-purposes. As discussed in Chapter 8 on governance, Shearing has proposed that police commissions and boards become policing commissions and boards, playing a regulating and coordinating role between public and private policing, and even allocating funds in ways that recognize that public police do not have a monopoly on issues of safety and security. That kind of role was recommended for the policing authority in Northern Ireland, and this approach was proposed by Sir Ian Blair, former commissioner of the Metropolitan Police at Scotland Yard, London as a way to co-ordinate public and private police. It may be one of the ways in which the *Private Security and Investigative Services Act* in Ontario, mentioned above as one control on private policing, gets extended in the next decade.

3

MEASURING POLICE EFFICIENCY AND PRODUCTIVITY

MEASURING POLICE EFFICIENCY OR PRODUCTIVITY IS VERY DIFFICULT, NOT LEAST of the reasons being that the job is so badly defined, and given the unquestioning way that politicians have been willing to fund police forces, little energy is devoted to finding adequate measurements of police effectiveness. Most measurements seem to relate to crime and criminal charges, and none relate to conflict resolution, guaranteeing civil rights, or assisting those who can't look after themselves.

The most frequently used measurement of performance is the clearance rate, that is, the number of crimes considered resolved or disposed of with some finality. Once an occurrence is resolved, it is considered cleared. Thus the Peel Regional Police, in its 2006 Annual Report, state that 56 per cent of crimes were "solved" in 2006, varying from 79 per cent of violent crimes to 35 per cent of property crimes. In its 2007 Environmental Scan, Calgary police note "overall clearance rates have remained steady at around 69 per cent for the past five years."

But these measurements mean almost nothing. Police lay three or four charges against most individuals in any single serious incident, and if the incident is resolved in some way, all charges are cleared. Sometimes the resolution is a court decision, which may be acquittal or conviction, and either decision results in a clearance. Sometimes complaints and charges are withdrawn, and that action clears the charges as well. A charge is also considered cleared if an officer deems it insolvable. Often the police are unable to find someone to charge for a crime, but if the case stays on the books, it is not cleared. The clearance rate does nothing to measure the effectiveness of detective diligence or police hard work. Clearance rates are not a helpful assessment of any police activity.

Another measure of performance often used is response time, that is, how quickly police respond to a call for service. The assumption is that the faster the response, the more efficient the police are, and the more likely they will be able to intervene and make an arrest. But this standard is not useful, either. Victims of crimes rarely call police as a first step, instead turning first to family, friends, and neighbours for support. Even if police arrive promptly, a considerable time has usually elapsed since the incident. Nevertheless, most police forces establish response time criteria for several types of incidents, with crime against the person the one receiving top priority.

The Toronto Police Service states that Priority 1 calls should be responded to within six minutes, but only 42 per cent of responses complied with the requirement. The immediate assumption from this information is that the police are not doing their job efficiently, even though speedy responses don't necessarily result in better outcomes. Toronto police officials suggest the way to deal with the problem is to lengthen the response time period, which would substantially improve compliance rates. But improved compliance rates do not yield better results either. Perhaps police could improve service expectations by being realistic with callers, stating when they will be able to arrive.

Several other standards are used to measure police effectiveness, but they do not relate directly to crime. One is the population served by each police officer. Why this ratio is important is unclear, except that it serves the argument that a city needs more (or, very infrequently, fewer) police officers. Such a figure reflects not much more than historic policing levels in a particular locale. Montreal has a population of 425 per officer, Halifax and Vancouver 450, Toronto 474, Winnipeg 509, Regina 528, Edmonton 544, Calgary 630, Ottawa 694, Quebec City 727. Varying ratios of officers to population do not relate to differing crime rates, as can be seen from the data in Chapter 1. And, as already noted, regardless of population served by each officer, in Canadian cities in general the average number of arrests by each officer is seven to eight a year.

If the decision was made to settle on the figure of 700 residents for every officer (a figure close to Ottawa's), would safety begin to unravel in places like Toronto, or would the world simply go on much as it does, with the only change being lower costs to the taxpayer? Local governments often make financial decisions that result in a loss of staff for municipal programs, but not for police, and thus we have no good example of what a reduction in police services and personnel would actually mean. Interestingly, 186 police officers per 100,000 people in Canada is similar to the number found in Scandinavia and Japan, but considerably fewer than that in the United Kingdom (258) and the United States (326).

Related to the number of personnel is the per capita cost of the police service: in 2006 it was about $320 in Toronto and Vancouver, $272 in Edmonton, $260 in Montreal, $245 in Calgary and Winnipeg, $217 in Ottawa, and $192 in Quebec City. Cost per capita bears little relationship to officers per hundred thousand population, so the usefulness of this measurement is not clear. The real issue, at the end of the day, is value for money. The cost per employee in 2009, both uniformed officers and civilians, is well over $100,000 a year, a sum that includes salary, pension and benefits, uniform and equipment, including radio, car, gun, and so on. The amount spent on public policing in Canada in 2005 was $9.2 billion, compared with $3.5 billion twenty years earlier, which in real terms is a 50 per cent increase. Just under 60 per cent of this amount was for municipal police forces, the remainder divided about equally between provincial forces, and federal and RCMP costs.

Another measurement, not frequently used, is the number of calls for service per officer. This measurement directly links the calls placed by the public for police help to the number of uniformed officers. As many have pointed out, 911 emergency services are considerably misused, often by callers with just a simple question for the police. In Toronto in 2007, about half the calls to police were ones that police felt did not require a service response. Some 1.8 million calls were received, and officers were sent out to respond to 925,000 of them. There were about 5,680 uniformed officers on the Toronto force in 2007, and each worked about 220 shifts. On average, then, each officer responded to slightly less than one call per shift. Similar patterns are seen in other large cities. Calgary police responded to 218,000 calls in 2006. With 1,640 uniformed officers working 220 shifts, on average each officer responded to two calls every three shifts.

Much time is spent on each call. In 2007 Toronto police spent 470 minutes (almost eight hours) of officer time on each Priority 1 call, usually with two or three officers together each spending several hours in attendance. This amount of time has more than doubled since ten years ago, when it was just over three hours. Other service calls in 2007 took, on average, just under three hours of police time. For traffic accidents, Toronto data in 2007 indicated that 4.4 hours of police time were spent on each personal injury accident, up from 3 hours ten years earlier. Just over 3.5 hours of police time was spent on each property damage accident, up from 3 hours ten years ago. As the 2008 Environmental Scan of the Toronto police service, which contains this data, notes, "the increase in time ... could represent an undesirable trend that may be indicating less efficient methods of investigating traffic accidents." Some might ask whether the amount of time of police attendance at an incident is simply expanding to fill the time available.

Another measurement of productivity is the quota system. Police officials generally state that officers are not given quotas for the number of parking tickets they are expected to issue each week or month, or the number of offences for moving-traffic violations. Members of the public claim to have direct experience to the contrary, stating that toward the end of each month officers seem to be much more diligent about issuing tickets, as though they are filling a quota.

One of the few confirmations of the existence of a police quota occurred in Toronto, and it received public notice because of a disciplinary hearing in December 2006 involving charges of insubordination against two police officers. The hearing officer, one police Superintendent Tweedy, made note of the acrimony between two officers, Sergeant Shawn Elliott and Officer David Deviney, that probably led to the incident on which the insubordination charge was based. Superintendent Tweedy stated, "Their platoon commander, Staff Sergeant Jack Kelly, had instituted a practice of encouraging his officers (in 23 Division) to write 25 traffic tickets during a work shift and then as a reward, allowed the successful officers to go home before the end of their assigned duty. The practice became known as the '25 and out' practice."

Deviney, a thirty-year veteran, refused to participate, saying the practice was unethical, and he is said to have reported the matter to the Internal Affairs department of the police. Staff Sergeant Elliott responded, according to Tweedy, by telling Deviney's colleagues that they should not speak to, socialize, or golf with him. Elliott claims that on May 2, 2005, he told Deviney to write an occurrence report on an event during which apparently nothing happened. Deviney and his shift partner said no such order was given, but Elliot brought the charge of insubordination because his order had not been followed.

Superintendent Tweedy decided on the basis of evidence at the hearing that Elliott had not given such an order. The charges of insubordination were dismissed. (This story provides insight into the sorry state of day-to-day management of the Toronto police force at the time.)

Superintendent Tweedy then commented on "25 and out:"

I must state that if the '25 and out' practice is still an existing practice, I direct that it cease immediately. I find it is an affront to the public interest and cannot be condoned as legitimate law enforcement behaviour, where quotas and personal benefit influence the day. It is but a sad example of unacceptable conduct undermining discipline, undermining unit cohesiveness, and contributing to a compromised management and work environment.

The situation raises many questions. The Toronto Police Accountability Coalition specifically asked how long the program was in place; whether other divisions employed similar quotas and rewards; whether Staff Sergeant Eliott was disciplined for employing such a program; and what happened to Deviney's complaint to Internal Affairs. Answers to these questions were never provided. Also unanswered is why management invested so much time and energy in pursuing this charge of insubordination that proved to be unsubstantiated and in any case was exceptionally minor.

One last way to measure productivity is to assess the public's perception of safety and fear of crime. It can be done by a public opinion survey, and most large police forces retain companies to conduct such surveys regularly. Statistics Canada data reveal that more than 90 per cent of Canadians feel safe from crime, and almost the same percentage feel they are receiving satisfactory police services. Nevertheless, about two-thirds of Canadians express a concern about crime, and almost one-third fear they could be a victim of crime in the coming year. Would these figures change if crime did not so occupy news and entertainment coverage in the media? In any case, it is difficult to relate perceptions to the way local police services are delivered.

Two examples of police work have already been mentioned, namely, making arrests and responding to calls for service, which, as noted, occupy only a small amount of an officer's time, raising the question of how a normal officer spends a normal shift.

The best study of day-to-day police work was done by the criminologist Richard V. Ericson and his colleagues regarding shifts in the 1970s. Ericson worked with the Peel Regional Police Force in a suburban community of about 300,000 residents in the Greater Toronto Area. Using students who spent shifts in police cars, Ericson was able to understand what happened on a regular shift. He found that on average an officer could expect to make two minor citizen contacts during a shift, as well as a more serious contact once every second shift. The minor contact would involve talking to citizens or dealing with a problem for a period ranging from a few minutes to about half an hour, averaging fifteen minutes each. More serious contacts would involve more complex encounters, perhaps resulting in a summons being issued, an arrest made, or the writing of an occurrence report. The more serious contacts would take on average forty-five minutes. Ericson also found that during an average shift an officer could be expected to make one property check such as following up on a reported burglary alarm or looking at a property on a random basis. He found that during an average shift an officer would write an occurrence report setting out the details of an event.

Ericson found that accounting for activities (such as those described above) occupied about two and a half hours of each shift. For the remainder of the time the officer was simply on hand, not having contact with any member of the community. He notes,

> The bulk of the patrol officer's time was spent doing nothing other than consuming the petrochemical energy required to run an automobile and the psychic energy required to deal with the boredom of it all. While this work may serve to order the population, it hardly brings personal dignity to anyone involved. The question remains whether the work is worth doing with such intensity at all.

Ericson also reviewed the work done by detectives of Peel Regional Police over a period of 179 shifts. He broke down the workload to show that 22 per cent of a detective's time was involved in case investigation, including interviewing complainants, witnesses, and informers. About 10 per cent was spent investigating and interviewing suspects and processing the accused. Another 22 per cent was spent on miscellaneous activities including those not related to police work. He found that about 46 per cent of a detective's time was spent in the office on matters not involving case investigation or suspect investigation. Ericson thought that this large amount of time was spent by detectives reporting to their superiors on what they did the other half of their time.

It would be very useful if more recent data on the actual work the police do were available. Nevertheless, it is probably fair to say that Ericson's findings still provide a useful picture of the current work of police officers. There may be some officers who for whatever reason find their days filled with interesting encounters with the public in the process of serving and protecting or maintaining law and order, but these officers would seem to be the exceptions. Apparently many officers have very little to do during their normal shifts.

Little crime is discovered by police acting on their own; most is brought to police attention by members of the public. A key factor in solving crimes is not learning a set of facts as much as identifying a suspect, and in almost every case identification is made not by the police but by a member of the public. In addition, it is more effective for police to start with a suspect in mind and work back to sort out the connection to the crime event than it is to start from the crime event and use what's learned at the scene to establish a suspect. It is always easier to make sense of events once the outcome is known and almost impossible to predict what will happen next. Most of the world works this way and makes decisions in this manner: detectives are not being unreasonable in using the same method. This reality of course runs contrary to the storylines of detective novels and television programs, which develop from the notion that little pieces of evidence lead to suspects. Detectives try to make sense of what happened by assuming they know who the suspect is. There is no question that the practice can and does result in inaccurate conclusions and in the conviction of innocent people, but it is about the only feasible way to proceed. The balances built into the criminal justice system, including the need for a prosecutor to provide proof beyond a reasonable doubt, attempt to overcome such assumptions, and mostly they do. But the existence of organizations such as the Association in Defence of the Wrongly Convicted, and the stunning reversals it and others have achieved in cases where courts have wrongly convicted suspects, show the heavy costs that are paid by some for this way of proceeding.

Studies reveal that the manner in which criminal investigations are organized and the relative heavy or light caseloads of detectives have little effect on outcomes or the number of crimes solved.

It is also evident that police patrol is not effective at uncovering crime. No matter how much police patrol, they are almost never on the scene of a crime even if it occurs on the street. One of the most common crimes is assault—that is, young men fighting each other—and about half occur on a street or in another public place, yet police patrol discovers not quite 4 per cent of assaults. Patrol work puts officers in the vicinity of crimes such as robbery, burglary, and vehicle theft less than 1 per cent of the time. Furthermore, rates of arrest for even serious crimes are quite low. In the United States, for instance, in the case of serious assaults, arrests are made in no more than one in six cases. Arrests are made in fewer than one in twenty cases of burglary, and one in ten cases of stolen vehicles. The obvious conclusion is that as an organization the police are not particularly effective crime fighters, though that ineffectiveness may have nothing to do with the way they do their work.

About two-thirds of police resources are invested in patrol—making police generally available and visible in the community—mostly by automobile but sometimes on foot. The rationale for patrol is that police visibility is in itself a deterrent to crime and makes people feel safer. Considerable evidence suggests that neither assumption is true, and that patrol is not a good use of police resources. A famous experiment took place in Kansas City in the early 1970s. Five different police beats in Kansas City were each divided into three groups. In one group, routine patrol ceased and officers responded only to calls for service. In a second group, routine patrol continued. In a third, routine patrol was doubled or tripled. At the end of the experimental period it was found that the strength of random patrol did not affect crime rates, arrest rates, or the public's fear of crime. The study has been criticized in terms of methodology, but it has never been duplicated; nevertheless its conclusions are now generally accepted by academics and police professionals. It has led to other methods of patrol, such as community policing, which will be discussed in a later chapter.

For many police departments, patrol takes place with officers in pairs during evening and nighttime hours. The Toronto Police Association advanced the idea of two-man cars in their contract bargaining during the late 1960s, and when management turned it down, the association filed a grievance, arguing that two-man cars were required for officer safety. The matter went to arbitration, and an arbitrator imposed the system on Toronto management for evening and nighttime hours. Many other forces (but not the RCMP) then implemented two-man cars. Obviously, two-man cars are far more expensive than cars with a single officer, and according to a 1976 study, they are more dangerous. Two officers tend to be more careless than one in dangerous situations, and they often fail to seek the extra help that might be needed, deciding to handle things on their own.

Journalist Malcolm Gladwell notes, quoting a third party, "'All cops want two-man cars. You have a buddy, someone to talk to. But one-man cars get into less trouble because you reduce bravado. A cop by himself makes an approach that is entirely different. He is not as prone to ambush. He doesn't charge in. He says, "I'm going to wait for the other cops to arrive." He acts more kindly. He allows more time.'" Reverting to one-man cars would clearly be a benefit to taxpayers and the public at large, but no police association has shown interest in reducing its ranks by 20 per cent, which is about the extra number of officers required to staff two-man cars.

One problematic aspect of police work is that it must be done in shifts, since a police service must be available twenty-four hours a day, seven days a week. Forces have different shift schedules, depending on the size of the force and the size of the area being policed. The simplest shift arrangement would be to divide the twenty-four hours into two periods of twelve hours each, with three platoons overall, two platoons each working twelve hours, while one is off duty. But this gets complicated by the fact that officers are not expected to work for more than five days a week, and management must factor in holidays, some weekends off, sickness, injury, and so forth. By its nature complex, shift work requires that management and employee representatives negotiate arrangements secured in a collective agreement of some kind. That agreement may include features such as rewarding officers who have been on night shift (perhaps with an extra day off), and aggregating days off for officers.

Brian White, a former Toronto police officer who now advises forces on appropriate shift strategies, has looked at what's needed for shift schedules. He finds that if 100 officers are employed on a three-shift program—day, afternoon, and evening—there will be a maximum of 20 officers on duty at any one time. With 80 officers on three shifts, a maximum of 16 officers are available for duty; with 140, 28. If 100 officers are working two shifts (that is, twelve hours a day), then 25 are available at any one time, providing they are working forty-two-hour weeks. With 80 officers on two shifts, 20 officers are available; with 140, 35.

White has also found that few shift schedules are geared to times when police receive the most calls for service. Often police forces spread resources equally throughout the twenty-four-hour cycle, even though calls peak in the early evening, and there's usually little for police to do between the middle of the night and the middle of the morning. Part of the problem is that shift schedules are difficult to change through a negotiation process; furthermore, those appointed as managers rarely have the management skills to allow them to address this complicated problem.

The shift schedule of the Toronto Police Service indicates how complex these matters can be. The Toronto force is divided into five platoons. Three platoons work every day, and the other two platoons are off. The platoons work shifts of ten, ten, and eight hours, which means there are twenty-eight hours of policing paid for during every twenty-four-hour period. The logical assumption would be that the arrangement would ensure overlaps during peak times for police service needs—early evenings—but that does not occur. The overlaps occur during times of a lesser demand for police service. The overlap turns out to be a significant amount of wasted money—about 15 per cent of salaries for the force. The Toronto Police Association shows no more interest in changing this aspect of work than it does the requirement for two officers in a cruiser after 5 p.m.

Toronto officers work on a thirty-five-day cycle. For seven days, they work day shifts ten hours long, then get six days off. For the next seven days they work ten-hour evening shifts, then have five days off. For the next seven days they work night shifts of eight hours, then get three days off. So in any thirty-five-day period, an officer works twenty-one days and has fourteen days off. Then the cycle repeats. (It is unclear what the arrangement would be with twelve-hour shifts, but surely it would mean that because of longer shift hours, officers would have more days off than workdays in any cycle.)

One result of the existing schedule is that officers have a great deal of time available for other pursuits such as second jobs and/or paid duty work on construction sites, sports events, night clubs, and private parties. The opportunity for paid duty work because of the shift schedule meant that in 2006 Toronto officers collected almost $25 million in duty pay, and more than seven hundred officers in Toronto, normally paid up to $75,000 in salary, took home over $100,000 from policing duties.

Duty-pay work in other cities is much less lucrative, given that in other cities officers need not be the ones who direct traffic around construction sites. The total of duty-pay work in Montreal in 2007 was $2.3 million, Calgary $2.2 million, and Vancouver $1.3 million.

Another result of shift work is the quality of the job done. After eight hours, most hard-working employees will be tired and will look for down time for the rest of the shift, as probably happens in the shift overlaps. After a second day of ten-hour shifts, an employee is unlikely to be providing solid work to an employer. Long hours rarely represent public money well spent. Exhaustion never results in good, attentive work.

Moreover, the on-off shift plays havoc with community relations. How does an officer who does not return to a "normal" shift for four weeks maintain any reasonable relationship with any community, person, or issue? From a community perspective, shift work is dysfunctional. Emergency services like ambulances and fire departments might work well on such shifts, but police who are asked to create good continuing community relations are performing an important but not an urgent service. It is difficult to think of any other service industry that operates on these principles.

Like two-man police cars, shift work, or (as it is called in police jargon) the compressed work week, is an issue that relates directly to productivity and efficiency. Rarely does a force have a shift schedule that makes the most efficient use of resources and offers the best response to the public.

This chapter has raised a number of issues about the nature of police work and how it is carried out. It is fair to ask whether the public receives good value for the substantial public funds spent on policing. The question does not yield easy answers. Police organizations engage in very few experiments to determine how policing might be done better or cost less money, so there are few ways of measuring value for the work done. A private organization might be driven by a competitor to review procedures and activities, but public police have clear monopolies in the places where they work and suffer no such challenges.

4

RECRUITMENT, TRAINING, AND MANAGEMENT

POLICE FORCES IN CANADA SEE THE OFFICER'S ROLE AS THAT OF A GENERAL-ist. The view is reflected in the fact that all recruits go through a standard selection and training process, police departments do not hire special-ists as officers, and very little work is performed by specialists highly trained in one branch of police work. The idea that generalists should fill all positions seems unique to police organizations, and is not found in schools, hospitals, governments, or law firms.

Certainly, some officers take courses to learn about particular subjects in detail, but this is just an add-on to the generalist approach. Rather than retain specialists to deal with youth or domestic violence, for instance, police forces assign officers to these duties, then give the officers spe-cial training. Officers rotate through the special squads, then move on a few years later to something else, and new officers are brought in and trained. The common element of all specialized services in a police force is training as a general police officer.

Some specialized squads are nothing more than patrol officers used on specific assignments. For instance, many large-city police forces have squads that deal with gangs and guns, and those squads, though headed by police managers, often consist of officers brought in for one or more shifts to do patrol work and other tasks in defined areas. The Toronto Anti-Violence Intervention Strategy (TAVIS) consists largely of police officers who are assigned to flood particular divisions for several weeks in the hope that certain kinds of street crimes can be deterred by police presence. TAVIS relies on the availability of general patrol officers, not on any special skills. It is a program that concentrates more on focus than on specialization.

The same is true of detectives. The bulk of detectives are attached to and operate out of district offices, responding to events that the patrol officers encounter. As well, large forces have centralized detective units for such matters as homicide, fraud, drugs, and organized crime. Both kinds of detective units consist of officers assigned to such areas, who then receive special training to carry out their duties. Some officers remain in their squads for many years, and some move on. Particular police squads can be characterized as functional specializations, where general police work is focused on specific tasks. Squads do not consist of specialists. For instances, domestic squads are not made up of social workers who have become police officers: they consist of police officers who may have an interest in domestic issues and may have taken limited training in that area.

One of the complicating factors is the way an officer's role is conceived. Police officers are not really seen as employees, working under managers: they are really free agents working under the law, which surely explains why they are basically seen as generalists. The influential English judge Lord Denning makes the point in clear and simple language in a 1968 decision: "It is the duty of every chief constable to enforce the law of the land. He must decide whether or not suspected persons are to be prosecuted and, if need be, bring the prosecution or see that it is brought: but in all these things he is not the servant of anyone, save of the law itself. No minister of the crown can tell him that ... he must or must not prosecute this man or that one. Nor can any police authority tell him so. The responsibility of law enforcement lies on him. He is answerable to the law and the law alone."

Denning's principle has generally been adopted by police forces, and officers have been treated as free agents, with substantial independent authority. What this means is that officers have considerable flexibility in how they will enforce the law, which contributes to their role as generalists.

An argument could be made that keeping most officers as generalists performing general patrol duties is the best way of ensuring that if a large group of officers is needed on a moment's notice—for a riot, a disaster, a major crime event—they can be quickly mobilized. However, it is possible to think of other organizational models that allow the objective to be equally well realized (such as requiring all officers to be subject to calls for urgent mobilization whatever the training and organizational niche), and in any case such events are quite rare. The more likely reason for the common pattern is that police forces are led by individuals who have for virtually all their working lives existed within this kind of police force. That this is the case can be seen by a review of police recruitment and training procedures, through to police management.

When it comes to recruitment, the generalist approach underlies attracting new staff to police forces. Police across the country have a standard for hiring a generalist officer. Since the assumption is that if the "right" individuals are recruited, we'll have a better police force, police have put considerable resources into recruitment, even though there are significant questions about the validity of the assumption.

There is no shortage of recruits for positions on police forces, as evidenced by the number of commercial guides (six different books, each priced at over $50, were seen in a visit to a Toronto bookstore in 2009) giving candidates tips on how to succeed in the recruitment examinations. Police forces tend to seek young candidates (under twenty-five years of age) who are looking for a first serious job. It is most unusual for someone to be hired as a police officer mid-career, after holding another job.

The profile of the ideal candidate is so widely agreed on that in Ontario, with more than forty police forces, large and small, urban and small town, looking for candidates, a common selection system was designed by police representatives in 1998. Called the Constable Selection System, it assesses over 80 per cent of all applicants. The minimum requirements for application are fairly straightforward: Canadian citizenship or residency; at least eighteen years of age; completion of at least four years of high school or equivalent; and "of good moral character and habits, meaning being an individual other people would look upon as being trustworthy and having integrity." Candidates must also have a driver's licence with no more than six demerit points, a first-aid-training certificate, reasonable eyesight and hearing, and no criminal record for which a pardon has not been granted.

A suitable candidate makes application, accompanied by a fee of about $300 (2009), to the force he or she wishes to join. The candidate should first approach the force where she or he hopes to be employed to secure agreement that it will offer employment if the candidate succeeds in the recruitment process. Stage 1 of the assessment process, intended to measure deductive, inductive, and quantitative reasoning, includes a written test to determine coherence and clarity of expression and understanding, a medical test (of eyes and hearing), and a physical test involving a short run. Stage 2 comprises an interview and a background questionnaire about schooling, criminal record, personal habits, and so on. Stage 3 is a post-interview assessment by police that includes background investigation, credit and reference checks, and a standard personality test, after which the candidate may be offered a job.

What's clear about the process to this point is that it is not geared to hiring specialists. It gives no preference to specific skills related to interests, expertise, or even possible employment experience (such as social work, accountancy, or management), nor to ethnic background (which could contribute an understanding of certain cultures, languages, or religions), nor to gender. These are all aspects that any police force attempting to fairly represent the community it serves should be taking into account, to ensure that there are as many women as men in the police force, and to reflect the cultural mix of the community. Certainly, some individuals may be selected by police recruiters to go through the application process, but their special distinctions gain no status or priority.

Addressing this neglect is critical. There is strong evidence that individuals will apply for a police job if they think they will feel comfortable in the organization. Will a person of colour apply if the police force is known to engage in racial profiling? A British study has shown that "the significance and relevance of race relations to recruitment have been underestimated by chief officers." In Canada, most police forces are overwhelmingly male and white, which probably discourages those who are neither from applying. The Toronto force and some others across the country have attempted to counteract this homogeneity with some recruiters of colour, surely a step in the right direction to achieve a more diverse public police. However, without concerted efforts, the recruitment process will not change.

Similar circumstances to those in Ontario exist in the rest of the country. The hiring guides available at bookstores outline questions a candidate would likely be asked in assorted Canadian jurisdictions in the first stage of the process. The formats differ from province to province in minor ways, but all make the same attempt to determine principally whether the candidate is reasonably intelligent.

Police forces are pretty serious about recruitment and put considerable resources into it. The Calgary police force has a Direct Entry Officer program which fast tracks experienced candidates through the training period, and the Alberta government runs a Provincial Nominee Program which allowed the Calgary force to make conditional employment offers to foreign applicants. The Halifax Regional Police service also has a program for experienced candidates (such as those who have worked in the military), with an offer of shorter training periods. The Toronto

Police Service in 2009 had a recruitment staff (dealing only with recruitment processes and not any other human resources matters) of 47 uniformed officers and 22 civilians, at a cost of $6.6 million. The activities of this staff (including job fairs, testing, interviewing) resulted in the force hiring 450 officer recruits and 650 civilians in 2008.

Once a candidate is accepted by a police force, he or she is sent for training. Each province has a training facility for recruits, and there is some variety in the way they are conceived. Most training facilities are not related to other learning institutions, but a few, such as the Saskatchewan Police College in the University of Regina, are attached to universities, and the Justice Institute of British Columbia trains workers in the corrections field as well as police officers. RCMP training takes place in Regina.

In Ontario, training for all police recruits in the province takes place at the Ontario Police College in Aylmer, a small town south of London. The college has fifty permanent teaching staff, and trains fourteen hundred recruits a year in three-month sessions. It also runs a host of short refresher and other courses for officers with police forces in the province.

The basic constable course at OPC takes three months, and students live at the facility during that period. The course deals with practical issues such as the use of firearms, the use of force, driving, physical fitness, police drill, and defensive tactics. It also includes material of a more reflective nature, including relevant laws police are expected to enforce, anti-racism, community policing, domestic violence, and ethics. Students are provided with a resident handbook that outlines the rules of conduct, expectations, and services. The college has a dress code, and very specific requirements about hair. For men it states:

> *Hair will be taper-trimmed at the back, sides and above the ear; shaving of all hair is permitted; sideburns shall not extend below a line horizontally bisecting the ear and shall be squared off horizontally at the bottom edge and taper trimmed to conform*

to the overall hair style.

Moustaches: when moustaches are worn alone, the unshaven portion of the face shall not extend outwards beyond the corners of the mouth; moustaches shall be kept neatly trimmed and will not be greater than 2 cm (3/4 in.) in bulk; and will not extend below the corners of the mouth.

Beards: only full beards will be allowed; full beards must be worn with a moustache and kept neatly trimmed.

For women it states:

Hair: hair shall not extend below the lower edge of the shirt collar; braids if worn shall be styled conservatively and tied tightly; hair may be trimmed short; long hair shall be pulled back tightly and rolled into a bun; the bun shall be covered with a hair net to keep it neat in appearance with no loose ends hanging out or down.

Makeup shall be applied conservatively.

These standards must be maintained once the recruits become officers.

Students are tested and required to achieve a grade of at least 75 per cent.

Several aspects of the training at OPC are worth comment. First, the fact that the college is in a remote location and students live together over a three-month period contributes to learning their most emphatic lesson: that they are not like other members of society and are being trained to do something that other people know little about. This separation from mainstream society is one of the dominant features of police culture, and clearly it is inculcated into recruits in Ontario from the earliest stages. Second, the isolation creates cohesion among students. If you don't fit in, you will quickly leave the program. The sense of cohesion and reliance on others who are (becoming) police officers is also characteristic of police culture, and it too is inculcated from the earliest days. Third, students learn how to follow orders. Drills are commonplace, with students expected to do as they are told, and the rules they must follow regarding hair and dress make it clear that their individuality is limited. Once again, group purpose trumps individual aspiration.

These are very strong lessons for any student to learn about becoming a police officer in Ontario. They are probably the most important ones that the college wishes to teach, the "subjects" taught being secondary to this basic training. Nothing is so powerful as a training technique than isolating students for a period of time and subjecting them to a predetermined routine.

But is such a training process one that will create a police force of sophisticated, educated, and diverse officers? More likely—beginning as it does with selection criteria met by only a certain small section of society—it will result in recruits who all fit into much the same mould as the existing policing regime.

Alternative considerations for the development of a new kind of police force are possible. A beginning might be to assess a community's particular makeup and policing needs and relate the skills and talents of recruits to that assessment, rather than hiring generalists. Does the force need certain language skills? Understanding of certain cultural or religious groups? Skills at negotiation, financial matters, domestic problems, women's issues, drug use, crime analysis? Advertising for candidates with particular skills would result in very different kinds of candidates stepping forward.

Integrating training with existing post-secondary institutions would remove the emphasis on recruits as special, or different from the rest of society. Integration rather than separation is always a good thing. The presence of a broader educational community would also provide recruits with opportunities to meet romantic partners outside the small and contained police community.

Once recruits have successfully completed training at the Ontario Police College, they return to the police force that sponsored them, to be sworn in as officers. Most large forces offer training for new recruits so they fully understand how the force in which they are working operates, and its relations with other agencies. Some offer more extensive additional training. For those entering the Toronto force, more training is in store at its own school, the Toronto Police College. The college provides practical training, and, like the Ontario Police College, it also offers officers refresher training.

If the example of Toronto is any indication, training by local forces leaves much to be desired. In 2006 the City of Toronto auditor reviewed the operation of the school (then called C.O. Bick College, after a former commissioner), noting that it was the first time such a review had been done in Canada of police training programs. The auditor's conclusions are not encouraging. He found that no one person had overall responsibility for all police officer training in the service; that the training and education unit did "not appear to encourage innovation and creativity in the areas of identifying better practices;" that, contrary to the *Police Services Act*, officers did not receive use-of-force training every twelve months; that "officers who are not qualified, both in terms of rank and required training, are being inappropriately assigned as coach officers;" that officers were not being evaluated as teachers; that training requirements were not determined; that the usefulness of training was not evaluated; and so forth. The conclusion seems to be that police training has not been taken as seriously by police authorities as might have been expected or hoped.

Short courses offering specialized training over a few days are offered for existing police officers by police training institutions across the country. The courses deal with the full range of matters that police work involves on a regular basis. As noted earlier, the courses are created to better inform generalists who have been assigned for (what is typically) a short period of time, such as a few years, to a specific area of work. There is no attempt to train a person to specialize in that area of work.

The limited part that specialized knowledge plays in police work can be seen in the example of the Peel Regional police force. It serves about 1.2 million residents in primarily low-density suburban communities just to the west of Toronto. In 2007 about twelve hundred officers worked on general patrol out of divisional stations, and about four hundred officers were assigned to specialized units. Those four hundred were spread among more than seventy-five specialized units involving human resource issues, various kinds of crime (including homicide, robbery, Internet child exploitation, fraud), traffic services, hostage negotiations, the marine unit, family violence, the canine unit, the explosive disposal unit, fingerprint technology, and emergency planning. Some units were clearly staffed entirely by civilians (particularly information technology), though they were managed by uniformed officers. Some specialties have only one or two officers assigned to them. Officers work in each unit for a few years, then transfer to another unit and receive more training appropriate to the new unit.

The use of discretion, a key part of a police officer's life, might be considered an essential training subject, with officers taught how and why to make choices in difficult situations. Alas, no police force seems to acknowledge the importance of discretion, nor is its useful exercise addressed during police training. Discretion may be subject to abuse if it is not considered openly. Racial profiling, for instance, might be an example of the exercise of police discretion gone wrong.

Appointees to police management have, virtually without exception, served as officers and worked their way up. There is not a police chief heading any municipal police force in Canada who has not spent his (or very rarely her) whole life working in a police force, learning on the job the way police work should be done and how the force should be organized. Chiefs have a very narrow range of experience. In Western Canada it is common practice to require that an individual have worked with at least two forces before being appointed chief, but in the rest of the country, it is common for the chief to be appointed from within a force.

Appointment from within is how officers become managers. Unlike other public and private organizations, no police force has a practice of looking beyond policing to find a good manager. The assumption seems to be that police experience and culture trump any management ability, but managers from within usually come with baggage, often a command-and-control approach, which is not due to lack of education: many police managers today have university degrees and take courses to improve management techniques. In most cases the degrees have been earned while the person has been a police officer, so the academic knowledge is an add-on to police experience rather than deriving from a personal, hands-on challenge or a real-life model of how to do things differently. The cost of this approach is high, since it subverts the very kinds of managerial innovation that are needed. Most police training is designed to produce followers rather than leaders, and those who secure leadership positions do so because of their commitment to police practices and traditions. Those who favour change often discover that their future lies outside of a police organization.

Thus, it is not easy to be optimistic about the change a new chief can bring. Brian A. Grossman in his 1975 book, *Police Command: Decisions and Discretion,* notes that "most chiefs are grateful that they have at last made it to the top," and they "don't see their job as a challenge; they see it as a sinecure. They've made it to the top and they are not going to jeopardize their position by setting new goals and moving ahead." A study by the Police Executive Development Project at Pennsylvania State University in 1972 found that police executives "appear to have a greater lack of insight into their own limitations than the general population and greater social conformist tendencies than the population as a whole."

Police departments invariably use rules as the key management technique, and those rules are written in great detail into the regulations of the police force. Rules set out virtually all aspects of the way an officer is to behave. Since most police managers have so little managerial experience, they rely on the regulations for control and lay charges of insubordination and discreditable conduct against officers who disobey their commands. (One example of such a charge was laid against Officer David Deviney who rebelled against "25 and out", mentioned in Chapter 3.)

Criminologists have asserted that generalized police work (responding to calls, aimless patrolling, and generally being visible) does little to prevent or reduce crime, particularly after the Kansas City study of the early 1970s, which found that "varying the strength of random mobile patrol does not affect crime rates, arrest rates, or the public's fear of crime." One alternative is to ask police to engage in a new kind of specialization, for instance putting resources into crime analysis in order to determine where crime is occurring and to look at possible ways to prevent it. This approach is often referred to as "problem-oriented policing," and it appears to have considerable impact when undertaken, but police forces seem to have difficulty reorganizing themselves to this end. (Such issues are discussed more thoroughly in Chapter 11.) Where it does occur, crime analysis seems to be the result of eager local officers rather than the police force taking a strategic step to respond to work innovatively. The generalist tradition is powerful within police forces.

5

POLICE CULTURE AND ITS IMPACT

JOKES ARE TOLD ABOUT ACCOUNTANTS, DENTISTS, AND OTHERS IN PROFES-
sional positions, and we laugh because we share an idea, albeit fuzzy,
of a prototypical accountant, dentist, or lawyer. We ascribe certain
behavioural traits to accountants, as though there is an accountancy
culture that is a product of training, focus, and the kind of work they
are expected to do.

The idea of character and culture is even more pronounced among
police officers. As discussed in Chapter 4, a common recruitment process is used virtually across Canada, and persons not deemed by recruitment officers to fit their concept of a police officer are not accepted.
Recruitment is followed by a training regimen that reinforces fitting in.
Once finally accepted into the police force, the new officer feels continuing pressure by the police force to fit in or move on.

Officers work in tightly knit groups that are hierarchical in nature
and dominated by those at the top. They either conform to the role
determined for them or the role shapes them. Officers have a different
experience from accountants, dentists, or lawyers, who often practice
with much less peer pressure, even in large firms; police culture is more

obvious than that of most other occupations.

The criminologist Jerome H. Skolnick, who teaches at the NYU Law School, succinctly defines the characteristics of the police personality, remarking that the pressure of the job is a very strong influence. An officer's first duty is to enter into and deal with dangerous situations, as required. As already noted, officers are actually infrequently imperilled, but the possibility of threat is real and ever present. Furthermore, danger can erupt without warning, even in routine circumstances. "The element of danger seems to make the policeman especially attentive to signs indicating a potential for violence and lawbreaking," writes Skolnick in *Justice without Trial: Law Enforcement in Democratic Society.* "As a result, the policeman is generally a 'suspicious' person." Indeed, an officer is taught to be suspicious, and to be on the lookout for what might happen next.

The second important duty of an officer is to act from a position of power, as an authority. The police are often asked to bring order to a situation in disarray, to take control in the face of menacing, deviant, or unruly behaviour. They are called in when others can't deal with a situation, the ones asked to exercise authority.

Responding to danger and exercising authority together shape police personality and create police culture. Both duties are subject to volatile variability and unpredictability, requiring an officer for his or her own protection to maintain an attitude of detachment, suspicion, and cynicism—an expectation of the worst. In turn, the public perceives police officers as distancing themselves from people in general and from the social order. Officers react by seeking out their own.

Exercising authority also isolates officers. It often means upholding rules and laws by calling lawbreakers to order. Miscreants resent being caught out, as we all do, even when we receive a ticket for a parking or traffic violation. Rule enforcers are always disliked. Moreover, those relied on to uphold authority can become authoritarian, completing the cycle of isolation and suspicion.

Thus isolated from those they police, officers naturally bond with those who understand their predicament, namely, other officers, in order to create a safe and comfortable place for themselves. Police quickly fit into a culture of their own—they can rely on one another, trust one another, often at the expense of outsiders. This tendency explains why so many officers have spouses and close friends who are officers themselves—the culture encourages an environment where it seems few outside the police circle can be trusted.

What's more, when officers are not firmly rooted in the community being policed, the separate police culture gets even stronger. Many big-city officers live in the distant suburbs, but their job is to police the inner city, an area whose values they either don't understand or don't share, and the literal and figurative distances exacerbate tensions.

It is easy to understand how the pressures of danger and authority lead officers to believe they are different from other people, that they are the thin blue line protecting society from mayhem and anarchy. From that place, police can easily ascribe to themselves a sense of mission in the way they safeguard the social order, while lamenting that the public really doesn't understand what they do. Their cynicism is reinforced by the number of social misfits and failures they must deal with, and the fact that many small-time criminals are always trying to skirt the law. Being faced with such experiences on a daily basis means officers may adopt a conservative view of life, politics, and society.

The characteristics of police culture can be summed up this way: it encourages robust solidarity with other officers; it is isolated from other parts of society; it assumes importance for protecting social values as understood by police; it believes others do not have a real understanding of police work. For the obvious reason that officers think they are not understood, the culture resents civilian control. The belief is that filling senior positions from within is the way to ensure managers best serve the cause of policing. A relatively free hand in spending is desirable because, once again, politicians don't fully understand police work. The culture makes it very difficult to bring change to a police force.

We need to understand that the powerful social culture of police officers is not just of their own making: it arises from the work they are required to do. Its influence is augmented by the fraternal links they form for support and is solidified by the power of the group. Assuming that choosing better recruits, or putting recruits through different training will break down or replace the culture is folly. It is more likely that those who choose to stand outside the culture will not pursue careers in policing.

Police culture finds its most cogent expression when officers band together to protect their interest as employees. In some provinces—New Brunswick, Nova Scotia, Manitoba, Saskatchewan, and British Columbia—police are allowed to form a real union like others; elsewhere in Canada they are permitted only to form an association. The right to strike has not meant that police strikes are regular occurrences (legislation and practice often state that unresolved disputes will be settled by binding arbitration), and it seems there is little difference between police associations and police unions in terms of their activities: whatever the law prohibiting such actions, associations are quite capable of carrying out job actions not unlike those allowed unions. Thus, on several occasions, under the leadership of the Toronto Police Association, Toronto officers have, in aid of bargaining for higher wages and other job benefits, refused to wear the full uniform (substituting baseball caps for the regulation hat) and have refused to issue tickets for traffic and parking violations for weeks at a time. (The City of Toronto collects about $6 million a month from such tickets, so the public cost is substantial.) There have been threats to be laggard in respect to other law enforcement, though it is unclear how often officers have done this. During a strike in 1969 in Montreal, officers impounded cars of the provincial police, the Sûreté du Québec, as well as kidnapped some of its officers to ensure that they would not enforce the law in place of the city police.

One function of a police association or union is to represent members in work-related matters, such as for charges under police regulations for insubordination or discreditable conduct. Like similar employee organizations, the association finds and pays for a lawyer for a member. Other functions are bargaining for collective agreements or contracts and ensuring representation for members facing complaints, investigation, or legal charges. In Ontario the *Police Services Act* does not permit an officer to be fired when he or she contests criminal charges. The officer is simply put on leave with full pay, and some criminal cases are not resolved for six, eight, or even ten years, when appeals are fully exhausted, so there is substantial financial benefit to officers (and a great cost to the public) in having the association provide such paid legal representation for an all-out defence.

As with many other employee organizations, the effectiveness of the association is often largely the result of the quality of management. Good managers make workers happy so they need not rely on their organization, but with bad managers, employees seek the protection of a strong organization. Police forces are sorely lacking in good managers, given the process for choosing them only from within the policing community. Furthermore, before being appointed a manager, an officer will have been a member of the association or union, and many police associations include all but the most senior managers as members. Such a close connection between the rank and file and management clearly strengthens the hand of the police employee organization.

Police associations and unions also play a large public role. Most noticeable are the occasions where they organize a display of solidarity such as at police funerals and memorial days. At these events, thousands of uniformed officers from many police organizations march by like a large army. The show of force often drowns out any expression of grief, and that surely is the purpose: the police intend to make a public statement about their might and willingness to act as a unified group. The result is the intimidation of anyone (particularly public leaders) considering expressing criticism of police activities. Such an expression of potency and authority is unique in Canadian society, so it clearly represents an impressive tool in the hands of police organizations.

Police organizations can take actions that make them a political element to be reckoned with. Perhaps the best example comes from the country's largest police organization, the Toronto Police Association, after its president, Craig Bromell (1997–2003) met with the Los Angeles Police Association to learn about tactics to make his group more powerful. Bromell came back from those training sessions in the 1990s with two new programs.

One was the True Blue Campaign. Police organizations often run fundraising events, calling members of the public to ask them to contribute. The True Blue Campaign, begun in 2000, was different. It was a telephone campaign asking citizens to donate to the police association in return for a sticker placed on the donor's car to indicate support for the police. The association said some of the money raised would finance a drive to change the *Young Offenders Act* (which the association felt was too lenient on youth) and to create a national DNA bank of criminals. Many people concluded the police association was attempting to establish a protection racket—those without stickers would feel the full weight of the law and those with would see their parking tickets and minor traffic infractions overlooked.

The Toronto Police Services Board, which governs police activity. in the city, refused to acknowledge any problem, and only one elected politician, city councillor Ann Johnston, was willing to speak out. Newspaper editorials, however, were very critical of what the association was doing, and after several months of controversy the police association abandoned the True Blue Campaign.

But the strength of the association was apparent. The police services board never did pass a resolution on the issue. Apart from Johnston, other locally elected politicians felt too intimidated to speak out publicly against the program. The only body willing to deal with the issue, ironically, was the provincial government of Mike Harris, and its threat of legislative intervention was what finally saw the association pull back.

Bromell's next initiative was direct political action. In September 2003, a week before a provincial election, the association took out a full-page ad in the *Globe and Mail* with the headline: "The Toronto Police Association Board of Directors proudly endorses Ernie Eves and his fellow Progressive Conservative candidates."

The ad included a smiling photo of Eves, the police association logo (a maple leaf, the CN Tower, and the scales of justice, with the words *Duty, Truth, Honour*), and a Toronto police car. Small type explained why Eves and his team should be supported. Conservative candidates in the Toronto area were listed, and in big print at the bottom was the reminder "Help Keep Ontario Safe. On October 2nd, vote for Ernie Eves and the P.C. Candidate in your riding." Closely related to such support were the actions of Toronto Police Chief Julian Fantino. Several years earlier, Fantino had made a point of being publicly visible at fundraising events for Mike Harris, then premier and leader of the provincial Conservative Party.

Section 46 of the *Police Services Act* states that "no municipal police officer shall engage in political activity, except as regulations permit." Regulation 554/91 says that police officers can express views on any issues "as long as the police officer does not, during an election campaign, express views supporting or opposing a candidate in the election or political party that has nominated a candidate in the election." An exemption is provided for an officer, not in uniform, engaging in these activities on his own time. In addition, Section 74 notes that "a police officer is guilty of misconduct if he or she contravenes Section 46," namely, the section prohibiting political activity. The law seemed clear.

Directors of the Toronto Police Association, elected by the rank and file, are police officers on leave from the force to perform their duties with the association, with the right to return to the force when their work for the association concludes. Are they "police officers" covered by the regulation? And does an action on behalf of uniformed officers fall within this legislation?

The acting chair of the police services board in 2003, Councillor Gloria Lindsay Luby, stated that there was nothing to be done since she believed board members of the police association were not police officers. The Law Union of Ontario wrote Chief Julian Fantino on October 2, asking him to investigate the matter, enclosing an opinion written by Albert Cohen, then city solicitor for Toronto, that directors of the police association were indeed police officers. Bromell, as president of the Toronto Police Association, responded that he intended to have the association endorse up to fifteen candidates in the November 2003 Toronto municipal election.

The police services board then sought three legal opinions. All three supported the view that members of the executive of the police association were police officers and therefore prohibited from endorsing candidates. Finally, in 2004 the board decided that "the endorsement or opposition of political candidates by municipal police officers is prohibited by the *Police Services Act* and its Regulations." The board ordered the chief to reiterate to officers that they are prohibited from using their status as police officers to endorse or oppose candidates during an election, and to discipline any police officer who contravened the policy.

In the case of the True Blue Campaign and the advertisement of Ernie Eves, the police association tested the limits of its influence to intervene in the political life of the city, and though the initiatives were abandoned, very contentious issues were raised. What is an appropriate role for police officers acting as a group in a democracy such as Canada? A police state is one where police abandon any thought of political neutrality and intervene to secure an end they desire, either for their own interest or for larger political interests. In Canada it is usually assumed that police officers are servants of the state and not its master. Was the association stepping over the line in these cases? If the association had persisted in its actions, would people of other political persuasions have found that police services were not available to them, or, more subtly, would they have feared that police would have discriminated against them? For instance, would a political candidate or supporter of a political party other than the Conservatives have thought an officer was pulling him over and giving him a ticket simply because of his political affiliation? Clearly, it is most important that to achieve good and fair policing police officers not be allied with political interests and not be seen to be so allied. Apparently in the first years of the new millennium the Toronto Police Association had no qualms about such connections. The police culture of solidarity at all costs prevailed over the independence expected of the police.

It is also important to be aware of the role police culture can play in provoking deviant behaviour in officers. One factor here is solidarity among officers, which seems to lead them to report exactly the same take on events in which they participated, even if it appears clear that the police version is inaccurate. A frequent claim is that officers get together to decide what to write in their notebooks about an occurrence in order to ensure that they are protecting fellow officers. Many forces now require officers to write in pen, not pencil, so notes once written cannot be changed. The claim of making common ground on evidence is difficult to prove, and it may not be true. But some possible examples have come to light.

One occurred after the tasering and death of Robert Dziekanski in Vancouver International Airport, when the four RCMP officers involved apparently talked about what they would write up in their notebooks about the event. Another occurred in Halifax in 2007, when a mentally ill man, Howard Hyde, was tasered and later died. Officers were unable to explain why their reports on the incident contained identical words, although they denied that their reports had been "doctored." Another occurred in Toronto in 2003. An officer asserted that Said Jama Jama, a teenager, attacked him in an Etobicoke mall parking lot, and the officer charged Jama Jama with police assault. Two other officers were present and recorded the same account in their notebooks. All three gave sworn testimony to this effect at Jama Jama's trial. At its conclusion, Jama Jama's lawyer unexpectedly showed the court a videotape taken by an unrelated person that evening in the parking lot, showing the officer making an unprovoked assault on Jama Jama. The judge immediately dismissed the police assault charge and laid an assault charge against the officer. The officer was convicted and sentenced to a brief period in jail. The officer, with the resources of the police association (and of course receiving full pay while on leave from the force), appealed. The appeal was dismissed some two years after the event, and the officer began serving his jail term, at which point he was dismissed from the force. Perhaps of equal interest is the fate of the two officers who clearly lied both in their notebooks and in their sworn testimony to the court. Several attempts were made to get information from police management about what disciplinary action was taken against the two, but no information has been forthcoming. The concern is that they continue to be employed by the Toronto force, as though what they did was nothing more than supporting their fellow officer.

The ubiquity of the video camera and cellphone with camera has resulted in more examples of misconduct by officers coming to light. As well, there are other examples of officers in attendance at police-related incidents but no one seems able to identify the officers who took improper actions. For instance, in Mississauga in August 2006, Orlando Canizalez and Richard Cimpoesu videotaped several dozen off-duty Region of Peel officers who were partying behind a strip mall. They claimed that they were roughed up by those officers when they refused to turn over their videotape. It proved very difficult to find officers willing to identify anyone present or anyone who participated in the assault.

It is very unfair to pretend that most officers tailor their evidence to protect their fellows, but the culture creates strong pressures, and speaking out against colleagues can lead to ostracization. The potential for bad behaviour devolves from the culture.

Another negative consequence of attachment to the culture is the misuse of police authority. Examples include arresting young students at a demonstration on the basis of spurious information, ticketing or laying charges against people because of ethnicity and/or colour (a subject to be dealt with in the next chapter), and the strip search: though the Supreme Court of Canada has stated that strip searches should be done rarely, in Toronto about one-third of those arrested are subjected to them. These are all instances of what Skolnick would call police justice without trial. Similarly, randomly stopping and frisking youth (particularly youth of colour) is also contrary to what the law permits to police officers, but it happens all the time, as noted in Chapter 6. Such examples of structured organizational deviance are generally seen by officers as the appropriate way to act in certain situations, and there is a confluence of organizational culture and police culture, hence the term *organizational deviance.* Some claim that inappropriate actions are the result of "bad apples," but the issue is not bad officers; rather it is the pressure of the police culture. Deviance breeds more deviance, so it becomes the practice of the organization.

Clearly this is an issue for management. It will require innovative approaches to the structure of police work and the tasks officers are expected to carry out. Rarely has effective, transformational leadership been available. As noted, police managers tend not to be good ones since virtually all were once foot soldiers who have moved up through the ranks and are bathed in the culture they are asked to manage.

6

RACIAL PROFILING

THE TERM "RACIAL PROFILING" WAS CREATED IN THE UNITED STATES IN THE late 1980s as a way of describing why police arrested more black people than whites. The implication was that police assumed blacks were more likely to be involved in criminal activity than whites, so they arrested them much more often. One cogent definition states that racial profiling "is best understood as a current manifestation of the historical stigma of blackness as an indicator of criminal tendencies." In a 1999 Ontario Court of Appeal case, *R. v. Richards*, Mr. Justice Marc Rosenberg refers favourably to the following definition: "Racial or colour profiling refers to that phenomenon whereby certain criminal activity is attributed to an identified group in society on the basis of race or colour resulting in the targeting of individual members of that group. In this context, race is illegitimately used as a proxy for the criminality or general criminal propensity of an entire racial group." In the past, it was simply called racial discrimination, but whatever name is attached, it targets appearances and not behaviour.

Obviously, the cause is racism, which has a long history in Canada and elsewhere. Slavery was a fact of life in Canada until 1792, when John Graves Simcoe, lieutenant governor of Upper Canada, stated that though existing slaves would continue in their status, no one could be newly enslaved. Slavery was not banned for another four decades. Aboriginal peoples were discriminated against from almost the earliest interactions with Europeans, and the *Indian Act* passed in 1876 confirmed their separate status; discrimination has continued virtually unfettered since then. A head tax was imposed in 1880 on persons arriving from China, and the Chinese were actually barred from immigrating to Canada from the 1920s to the 1940s. Many other instances of institutional racism could be cited. Only with the passage of human rights legislation in the late 1950s did racial discrimination become prohibited, even if it continued to be practiced because of long habit.

Countless examples of racial profiling by Canadian police officers are available, but perhaps a study done in the mid-sized city of Kingston, Ontario, by one police force into its own activities is the most helpful illustration. The study was ordered in 2003 by the chief of police, William Closs, after a disturbing incident of racial profiling by his officers. Closs retained Professor Scot Wortley of the Centre of Criminology, University of Toronto, to conduct the study.

Between October 1, 2003, and September 30, 2004, all officers were asked to fill out a contact card every time a citizen was stopped by police and questioned in anything other than a casual manner. The contact card would contain relevant information about location, reasons for the stop, final disposition, as well as the age, gender, and race of the individual stopped. The information was then entered into a computer for analysis. The year produced data on just over ten thousand stops, or just over one stop per shift for each officer, which is about standard for Canadian urban police forces. About two-thirds of the stops were of pedestrians, one-third of people in vehicles. For every 91 individuals with white skin who were stopped, police stopped 126 Aboriginals and 320 blacks. Some 92.7 per cent of Kingston's population is white, and 92.6 per cent of those stopped were white. Some 1.6 per cent of the city's population is aboriginal, but 2.2 per cent of those stopped were aboriginal. Some 0.6 per cent of the city's population is black, but 2.2 per cent of those stopped were black. Thus, blacks were almost four times as likely as whites to be stopped. The likelihood that a black youth between the ages of fifteen and twenty-four would be stopped was more than five times greater than a white youth in the same age range. Whites were charged or arrested in 6.2 per cent of stops, blacks 9.6 per cent, an additional indication of the discrimination faced by blacks.

In releasing the preliminary results of the study, Chief Closs put the findings within the larger context of data about racial profiling. He noted there had been "16 years of reports and commissions" in Ontario, and said the government had been "non-committal on the issue of biased policing and data collection." He specifically cited the Race Relations and Policing Task Force of 1989 (Ontario), the Commission on Systemic Racism in the Ontario Criminal Justice System from 1992 to 1995, the 2003 Ontario Human Rights Commission report, "Paying the Price: The Human Cost of Racial Profiling," and the report of the inquiry into the death of Neil Stonechild in Saskatchewan in 1990. All reports make the evidence about the reality of racial profiling abundantly clear. Closs noted the difficulty of proving racial profiling by police: "The reality is that allegations of biased-based behaviour in police rarely, if ever, have been dealt with through the *Police Services Act*, because of the non-existence of real or physical evidence ... Unless captured by a hidden camera or 'sting' operation, there never is irrefutable proof of racial pro-filing: without evidence, there can be no misconduct charges under the *Police Services Act.*"

He went on to compare what has been done in Canada with actions taken in United States. "We do not always concur with the American model of policing, but I cannot emphasize enough the depth of commit-ment and the investment of energy that our counterparts in the United States have given to the matter of racial profiling." He noted that "Amer-

ican police chiefs have become comfortable with the notion of data collection with respect to bias-free policing," and unlike in Canada, where
the Kingston experiment was the first time such data collection had been
done in the country, it is common practice in American cities. He cited
an American police research group that stated that collecting data on
race/ethnicity "reflects accountability, openness and sound management." David Tanovich, a University of Windsor law professor, notes in
his 2006 book, *The Colour of Justice: Policing Race in Canada*, that this
data collection happens in forty-six of the fifty states in the USA.

Chief Closs provided the context required for a study of this kind, and
did so in a fair and comprehensive fashion. It was a class act by a police
chief on a controversial subject. Somewhat later, the chief held a press
conference, during which he tearfully apologized to people of colour in
Kingston.

But some were not impressed. The Kingston Police Association
responded that the data weren't true. The Canadian Association of
Police Chiefs said that Kingston had a problem it should address—as
though the issues raised by the data applied only to that city. Worse still,
the Kingston Police Services Board decided to take no further action on
the matter of racial profiling, as though the study had never taken place
and the data had never been gathered. No similar study has been done
by a Canadian police force since that time, though virtually every large
police force in United States collects such data regularly.

But the lack of action should not be taken as a sign that racial profiling
does not exist. In another study, Wortley found that "Blacks in Toronto
were twice as likely to report experiencing a single police stop, and four
times more likely to report experiencing multiple stops over a two year
period." He also found that "having a university degree does not protect
Blacks from police, as the level of education actually increases the likelihood of being stopped. The reverse was true for Whites." These findings generally confirmed what Wortley had learned in a study of about
thirty-four hundred high school students in Toronto in 2000, data that

showed black youngsters were stopped much more often even when they had not engaged in any kind of deviant or criminal behaviour.

Racial profiling was also the conclusion when the *Toronto Star* analyzed extensive data collected in the city. The *Star* obtained computer data from the Toronto police force on instances of police/citizen interaction from 1996 to 2002 when a person was charged with a crime or traffic violation. The data recorded some 480,000 interactions, or about 80,000 for each year. *Star* reporters, led by Jim Rankin, reviewed the information and published a series of articles in October 2002 summarizing what they had found. Black citizens, who make up about 8 per cent of the Toronto population, constituted more than one-third of all drivers charged with offences and one-quarter of all those charged with violent offences. Blacks arrested for simple drug possession were twice as likely to be taken to the station and detained as white suspects.

Julian Fantino, then Toronto police chief, responded, "There's no racism ... We do not do racial profiling." As he writes in his 2007 book, *Duty: The Life of a Cop,* "I said the *Star* had been very selective in the use of its data and didn't have all the facts ... In my view the paper had an agenda. They started out with some preconceived notion and then set out to prove it ... I thought their behaviour was irresponsible." Fantino continued, "You can't hide something as systemic as what the *Star* was portraying. I think this was the perfect example of the media creating a story and running with it. But the *Toronto Star* ... has never been a friend to me."

Norm Gardner, chair of the Toronto Police Services Board, called the *Star*'s allegations "reckless." Toronto city councillor and police services board member Gloria Lindsay Luby made similar denials. Toronto mayor Mel Lastman said, "Police only arrest bad guys ... I don't believe the Toronto police engage in racial profiling in any way." Craig Bromell, president of the Toronto Police Association, questioned how the *Star* had come to its conclusions since he said Toronto police did not do racial profiling.

The police services board then hired "a world-renowned expert on demographics" who said the *Star*'s conclusions were "junk science" and that the figures in the police database "were not designed for research." But the attempt to discredit the *Star*'s conclusions did not get very far, as other unrelated sources gave credence to the reality of racial profiling. By chance a case arose in the Ontario Supreme Court in which a judge dismissed charges of drunk driving because of racial profiling, and the Crown attorney involved agreed that racial profiling by police was a fact of life. The Ontario Association of Police Chiefs waded in to say, "These unsubstantiated allegations are extremely provocative and disturbing in their intent."

But then the deputy chief of the Ottawa police force found his remarks at a forum were quoted widely: "Our members are not racist … but we are no different than any other organization … Do stereotypes exist? Yes. Do things happen because we stereotype people? Yes. So if we are going to call that racial profiling, then yes, it certainly occurs in our police force as well as other police services."

The Ontario Human Rights Commission released the conclusion of an unrelated investigation it had just completed, stating that racial profiling existed. The report was titled "Paying the Price: The Human Cost of Racial Profiling." Chief Fantino again exploded and filed a Freedom of Information request to get the full names of those who had complained to the commission.

The Toronto Police Association undertook a class-action libel suit against the *Toronto Star* for $2.7 billion. The lawsuit was dismissed by the court, which said that there was no allegation about any individual officers, but rather that the *Star* had done no more than say that the evidence shows that racial profiling exists and steps should be taken to do something.

The issue dragged on, with more examples of persons of note agreeing to the reality of racial profiling, and police officials generally denying the same.

There was no good outcome from the articles in the *Star*. Although the Toronto Police Services Board made several decisions stating it is opposed to racial profiling, and though a new police chief, Bill Blair, expressed his opposition too, specific action such as the Kingston survey has never been undertaken.

In 2008 the *Toronto Star* asked for the computer data on police stops since 2002 so it could update the story. The Toronto Police Services Board refused to release the information. The *Star* took the matter to arbitration, where it won the right to obtain the information, but the board appealed the decision to the courts, where it was victorious, and the *Star* appealed. The request was finally dealt with by an Ontario appeal court, which ordered the police to release the data.

The *Star* published its analysis of the new information for the period 2003 to 2008 in February 2010. The data revealed that a person with black or brown skin was three times as likely to be stopped by police as one with white skin. About three hundred thousand contact cards were filled out for each year, though police state that a card is not always filled out when a contact is made or a person is stopped. The card registers the individual's name, address, skin colour, age, birthdate, time and place of stop, and reason for the stop. As was revealed in the 2002 data, persons with black skin received about three times as many tickets as those with white skin for such matters as driving while suspended, not carrying a licence, or failing to change the address on a licence; charges for violent crimes were 3.6 times higher; and when charged, blacks are held for bail about twice as long. It might be alleged that individuals with black skin are responsible for a lot more driving offences and crime than others— an allegation not borne out by evidence—but even if this were the case, it would not explain why, after blacks have been charged, police hold them twice as long as whites. The fact that police hold them longer can only be explained by officers treating individuals differently according to the colour of their skin.

But instead of denying that racial profiling occurs, as was done in

2002, the chief and other senior officers this time admitted that it happens, implied it's normal, and then explained why the police practice of carding blacks is not something to be worried about. ("Carding" is the name given to the practice of filling out cards that collect information about individuals who are of interest to the police.) One police explanation for the benefit of carding is that it provides a more rounded look at those stopped—who their friends are and where they were on a certain date, for instance. The police say they have used this information to solve crimes. Unfortunately, this is the classic story of the police deciding that to provide more safety they need a dossier on everyone who could cause trouble, and that means creating dossiers on young men with black and brown skins. In a 2004 Ontario court case, Justice Harry LaForme referred to carding—a "208 card," Toronto police call it—stating,

> *Although I do not dispute that 208 cards might well be a useful and proper investigative tool for the police, in my view the manner in which the police currently use them make them somewhat menacing. These cards are currently being used by the police to track the movements—in some cases on a daily basis—of persons who must include innocent law-abiding residents.*
>
> *One reasonable—although very unfortunate—impression that one could draw from the information sought on these 208 cards— along with the current manner in which they are being used—is that they could be a tool utilized for racial profiling …*
>
> *I make my observations only to express a profound note of caution. If the manner in which these 208 cards are currently being used continues, there will be serious consequences ahead. They are but another means whereby subjective assessments based upon race—or some other irrelevant factor—can be used to mask discriminatory conduct …*
>
> *This kind of daily tracking of the whereabouts of persons—including many innocent law-abiding persons—has an aspect to it*

that reminds me of former government regimes that I am certain
all of us would prefer not to replicate.

The other rationale given by the police was that it makes sense to stop more black and brown kids in neighbourhoods where there are shootings because they are the ones who are doing the shooting. When youths with those skin colours complain that they don't appreciate being stopped and questioned when they did nothing wrong, police imply those are just the breaks of the game. This kind of racial profiling after the fall of the twin towers in Manhattan on September 11, 2001, led to the wrongful arrest of many innocent Arab men of the Islamic faith. It also led to the "no-fly list," which arbitrarily identified individuals who should not be allowed on an airplane. A number of entirely innocent people who were included on that list have been unable to find a way to get their names taken off it. Tanovich referred to the carding experience in Toronto as creating a "no-walk list."

Racial profiling is being used by police to achieve something that discrimination will never achieve, namely, the reduction of violent and anti-social acts by youth. As many studies have shown, including *The Roots of Youth Violence* by Roy McMurtry and Alvin Curling, the solution lies in programs that improve the lives of youth and of their families. These are not problems police can solve. Young adults constantly discriminated against by the police who insinuate that they are not persons to be trusted are bound to become more alienated and angry. Discrimination is not a positive strategy for police to pursue.

Racial profiling has a significant impact on members of the force who happen to have the same skin colour as those profiled. Doreen Guy, a black police officer with the Toronto force, referred to this issue in her remarks to friends at her retirement party in February 2004: "Recently when the issue of racial profiling came to the fore through the article by the *Toronto Star*, many of us Black Officers felt tremendously encouraged because we felt that our concerns had be[en] legitimized and that the issue was now out in the public domain. We felt that, finally, the issue would have to be acknowledged and addressed ... I was dismayed by the Service's response to the report on racial profiling that was recently released. The Service's position seems to be that the majority of police officers are decent human beings and that maybe we have only a 'few bad apples.' As I said earlier, perception is everything."

Guy's retirement talk recounted a long and painful period of prejudice working for the force, until she was taken under the wing of the senior black officer on the force, Keith Forde. Her problems began when she "confronted a male officer who was making derogatory remarks and using a racial slur against young black males." She was then deemed not a team player. "No one wanted to work with me because it was said that if something happened I could not be relied on to 'back up.'"

As Norm Stamper, former chief of the Seattle police force, makes clear, such slurs are part of normal police behaviour. He relates a moving episode when he asked the only black officer on the squad about racial slurs, and "he fell into a silent weeping jag," which quickly turned into tears streaming down his face. As Cardinal Emmett Carter noted in his report on the Toronto police force in 1979, "The use of verbal taunts is far too prevalent. When a person is called a nigger, a queer, a faggot, a chink, a paki, usually with the appropriate accompanying adjectives, he has been attacked as surely as if he were struck." The cardinal recommended that the police chief order "in the strongest terms" that such language not be condoned. Concerns remain that slurs continue to be a regular part of police life, causing damage within and outside the force.

Blacks are not the only group subject to racial profiling: there are many examples of others with not-white skin who suffer because of racial profiling, particularly aboriginal people. There are many heart-rending stories about their fate in the hands of police, none perhaps as shocking as the case of Neil Stonechild in Saskatoon.

Saskatoon police had a practice they referred to as "the starlight tour." It involved seizing an aboriginal person in the downtown, and then driving him to the outskirts of the city and forcing him out of the car. This was what happened to Neil Stonechild, a seventeen-year-old aboriginal taken into a police car by Saskatoon police on a very cold night in November 1990, driven eight kilometres from the downtown to the edge of the city and forced out of the car. His frozen body was found five days later.

Police conducted a preliminary investigation that revealed a number of suspicious circumstances about the youth's death—marks on his wrists that might have been caused by handcuffs, a missing shoe—but the formal investigation, which was overseen by a staff superintendent, was superficial and was quickly closed. It was not until a public inquiry was held fourteen years later that the whole story spilled out—two officers had indeed seized him on the street, driven him to the edge of the city, and pushed him out into the very cold night. The officers and the force did all they could to obstruct those who wished to learn exactly what had happened. As the judge at the inquiry noted,

> In the years that followed, the chief and the deputy chiefs of police who successively headed the Saskatoon Police Service rejected or ignored reports from the Stonechild family members and investigative reporters for the Saskatoon StarPhoenix that cast serious doubts on the conduct of the Stonechild investigation. The self-protective and defensive attitudes exhibited by senior levels of the police service continued, notwithstanding the establishment of an RCMP task force to investigate the suspicious deaths of a number of aboriginal persons and the abduction of an aboriginal man. These same attitudes were manifested by certain members of the Saskatoon Police Service during the inquiry.

It is chilling to think that the Saskatoon police had regularized this racist practice against aboriginal citizens—one that led to at least one death, with strong evidence that there were others—by giving it a clever name, "the starlight tour." The denials that occurred in subsequent years speak to the prevalence of officers' going to extraordinary lengths to protect their fellows, including dismissing contrary evidence.

The availability of such widespread data on racial profiling requires that we confront some difficult questions. Are police generally racist? Is there something about the police culture that leads to racial profiling? The answers are not clear-cut, and of course whatever conclusions are reached will be general in nature, and not applicable to every single officer. Nevertheless, perhaps the best summary can be found in a 1992 report of the City of Toronto auditor:

> A change occurs after joining the force. There was significant evidence that many police officers who are constantly in contact with [the] public develop strong feelings and beliefs as to the attributes of individuals based on factors such as appearance and racial background. These officers would no doubt be offended if their attitudes were described as potentially racist. Nevertheless, the same attitudes can and do produce a bias in behavior which results in unequal treatment of individuals of different cultural or racial backgrounds.

Stamper is more straightforward and provocative: "Simply put, white cops are afraid of black men. We don't talk about it, we pretend it doesn't exist, we claim 'color-blindness,' we say white officers treat black men the same way they treat white men. But that's a lie."

Tanovich calls the North American "War on Drugs" a "War on Blacks," and produces compelling evidence to back up his claim, showing the substantial increase in the number of black persons charged since the War on Drugs was created in the mid-1980s, even though "no evidence shows that black people are more likely to use drugs than others or that they are overrepresented among those who profit most from drug use." He also argues that drug trafficking has been racialized, pointing to the case of Calgary officers who searched two Vietnamese men getting off a bus on the apparent assumption by police that Vietnamese men could be expected to deal in drugs. Judges across the country are now refusing to permit evidence to be introduced into court on the grounds that stops were made by police on the basis of racial profiling.

Devising a solution to the problem of racial profiling must begin with an admission that it occurs with regularity. The admission seems not to have been a stumbling block for most American police forces, but apparently it is in Canada. No police force has agreed to develop policies from the fact that racial profiling exists. Instead, most forces have taken the position that it is against policy, and have left the matter at that. Direct action (such as using the contact cards that collect personal information as the basis of new procedures) has not been forthcoming.

Stamper met with his officers and they formulated a host of approaches: modifying recruitment, testing and screening new officers with a better focus on racial attitudes; putting officers in plain clothes into social services areas in black communities for a few weeks; better analysis of individual and organizational patterns of discrimination; making supervisors investigate all instances of the rumoured use of excessive force; firing those who use racial slurs. He makes a number of recommendations for better training, as do many others, but there are questions about whether better training will be able to overcome the pressures of police culture. Training often seems like the easy response, when it appears to have little impact on the way a police force carries out its duties.

Christine Silverberg, former chief of the Calgary police force, has suggested that the basic problem with racial profiling and other police deviance is the command-and-control line of authority pursued by police forces. She argues for less-hierarchical rules, ensuring instead that officers understand and act on core values reinforced by good managers.

Tanovich cites the recommendation of the Aboriginal Justice Inquiry of Manitoba into the police shooting of J.J. Harper, a leader in the aboriginal community that the "Winnipeg Police Department cease the practice of using race as a description in police broadcasts." Police should instead simply refer to complexion as part of the description so that race would no longer be the dominant aspect of the description. Tanovich agrees that this will be effective only if the description is specific about other characteristics such as sex, height, build, age, hair, facial hair, glasses, and so forth. Given the varieties of skin colour now falling under the labels black and aboriginal, it is fair to say that though the proposal is not without its drawbacks, it would be one way of taking race out of everyday discussion by police.

Ideally, the more the officers of a police force reflect the diversity of the community it polices, the less it will engage in racial profiling. That may prove true, providing (as occurs in Canada's larger cities) a wide variety of racial and cultural groups is present in the population. Most police forces are now trying to become more diverse, as recounted in an earlier chapter, so the problem is what to do in the interim between the present and the future diverse state of police forces. Given the slow progress being made (a majority of new hires continue to be white and male), improvement will take a considerable period of time. Meanwhile, there are good reasons why visible minorities may not feel comfortable on a police force and thus be reluctant to apply. As Doreen Guy learned on the Toronto force, it's not much fun to be discriminated against at work and denied reasonable opportunities for promotion—hardly incentives for a member of a minority community to consider a career as a police officer.

7

COMPLAINTS ABOUT THE POLICE

In the early years of the new millennium, British Columbia had a complaints system that was no different from those of other police forces in the country. If you had a complaint, you took it to the police force. The force did its own investigation, and you then learned the result of that investigation. Concerns were expressed in that province with the system of police investigating themselves, and in 2005 former provincial Supreme Court judge Josiah Wood was asked by the British Columbia government to review complaints about several municipal police forces. Wood's study was released in 2007. It reviewed a random sample of 294 complaints from eleven independent municipal police forces.

Judge Wood's general conclusion was that "a majority of complaints were investigated in a manner that was reasonable and appropriate." But the optimism of that statement was undermined by the number and type of cases that were not investigated well. Judge Wood found that fifty-six investigations (18 per cent) did not meet the "reasonable and appropriate" test. Forty-nine of the fifty-six concerned serious abuses of police authority: thirty-six dealt with allegations of excessive use of force, five with allegations of wrongful arrest, and eight with allegations of wrongful search or seizure of property. In twenty of the complaints about excessive use of force by police, Judge Wood concluded that the "findings, conclusions, or recommendations were unreasonable or inappropriate."

He also found that of the ninety-four complaints of excessive use of force, in not a single case did the police investigators conclude that the complaint was substantiated. He said, "Investigators seemed reluctant or casual about investigations of potentially criminal misconduct by police officers." He found there were forty-six cases whose files were not forwarded to the Crown for criminal prosecution. And he found there were often unexplained delays or a lack of rigour to the investigations done by the police. He also stated, "The factor which caused me the greatest concern ... [was] the lack of complete acceptance by the police of the concept of full civilian oversight."

A similar kind of study was initiated by Paul Kennedy as commissioner for Public Complaints against the RCMP. The RCMP investigates complaints against its own officers, and the conclusions of those investigations filter up to Kennedy, who in turn reports to the RCMP commissioner, William Elliott. The commissioner has been known to change Kennedy's recommendations.

Kennedy reviewed 600 complaint cases across the country from 2002 to 2007, and filed his report, "Police Investigating Police," in May 2009. Some 150 of those cases were thought relevant to further review, and of those, 28 were investigated in detail. There were 14 cases of assault, 6 cases involving death, and 8 cases involving sexual assault. Kennedy found that in a quarter of the cases the primary investigating officer personally knew the officer being complained of, and in a few cases was from the same detachment. Some investigators had little training in investigation, and often only one investigator was used, even though general police practice is to use two officers when questioning someone. He found that 19 cases—that is, two-thirds of the total—were handled "partially or entirely improperly." Eight criminal charges were laid in 5 of the 28 cases, and three convictions were obtained.

Kennedy made a modest recommendation: in serious cases (such as those involving death), the investigation should be carried out by an independent police force. RCMP Commissioner Elliott rejected that suggestion. RCMP Superintendent Wayne Rideout did tell a public inquiry in September 2009, "We are not perceived publicly to be able to investigate ourselves," but his opinion was ignored, and Kennedy was forced out of his position with the RCMP by the federal government of Stephen Harper at the end of 2009.

Although these two studies are somewhat unusual—few governments have been willing to review how complaints against the police are dealt with—anecdotal evidence leads to the belief that the conclusions both came to are fairly standard and widespread. Having police investigate themselves seems not always to result in an account of what actually occurred.

An example from Toronto makes the point. In this case, three years elapsed between the filing of the complaints and their resolution. Complaints were filed by four teenagers after they were arrested at a demonstration in Toronto, held for up to nine hours in a police van, then released without charge. The complainants alleged misconduct on the part of the police inspector in charge of police actions during the demonstration. The Toronto police force investigated the complaints, found them without basis, and dismissed them. The teenagers then appealed the decision to the Ontario Civilian Commission on Police Services (OCCOPS), which has some jurisdiction to review the way police forces deal with complaints.

OCCOPS reviewed the complaint and reached a settlement between the parties. In August 2004, the Toronto Police Service issued a press release outlining the terms of the settlement. It stated:

> The parties hereby agree, on consent, and request that the tribunal dismiss the allegation of misconduct against Inspector Tony

Crawford. The parties agree to the following statement of facts that summarizes the circumstances that lead to the allegation of misconduct arising from a protest that occurred in downtown Toronto on October 16, 2001:

On October 16, 2001, a demonstration took place in downtown Toronto. In planning to police this event the Toronto Police Service drew in officers from surrounding police services. In all some 550 officers were deployed over a period of 16 hours. Forty arrests were made, although not all led to the laying of criminal charges.

Several months after this event four members of the public filed formal complaints about the treatment they received in the hours leading up to the demonstration. The complaints included concerns regarding the manner in which they were detained in a police prisoner transportation wagon. The citizens were detained in the wagon for periods of between 6 to almost 9 hours. Police wagons are not designed for detention for these periods of time.

The complaints were investigated and marked as "unsubstantiated" by the Toronto Police Service. The complainants sought a review of this decision by the Ontario Civilian Commission on Police Services, who ordered a hearing against Inspector Tony Crawford. Inspector Crawford had been the incident commander at the demonstration.

Here's what the parties agreed:

1. *Four public complainants, John Milton, Sarah Kardash, Adam Chaleff-Freudenthaler (16 years of age at the time) and Joshua Brandt (15 years of age at the time) were detained at the demonstration and confined in a police wagon for periods of between six to almost nine hours. Sarah Kardash was detained in the police wagon the longest time. [Pursuant to section 110(3) of the Youth Criminal Justice Act, Adam Chaleff-Freudenthaler and Joshua*

Brandt both waive their rights to non-publication of their identities. As such all information contained in this document may be published.]

2. *The conditions of detention in the police wagon were extremely uncomfortable due to the confined space, poor ventilation, excessive temperature, poor lighting, and lack of washroom facilities.*

3. *All of the public complainants were handcuffed with their hands behind their back for the entire period of detention, apart from John Milton who had his handcuffs changed to being cuffed in front of him as a result of his arms being in spasm for approximately half an hour.*

4. *The complainants were not provided with any food or water or with the opportunity to use a washroom, although Joshua Brandt and Sarah Kardash requested to do so repeatedly. As a consequence of Sarah Kardash being denied the ability to use a washroom, she was forced to urinate on the floor of the police wagon, which required the assistance of another female detainee.*

5. *All complainants were ultimately released unconditionally from various police stations without being charged with any offence.*

6. *In planning for the police management of the demonstration, the Toronto Police Service did not adequately anticipate or address the possibility that persons would be detained in police wagons for excessive periods of time. The Service did not adequately plan for the supervision of the management of persons detained in police wagons in order to avoid the possibility of excessive detention.*

7. *In light of the inadequate planning and supervision, the parties agree that the complainants were detained for an excessive length of time and under unacceptable conditions in the circumstances.*

The complaints have not gone unnoticed and the Toronto Police Service has now significantly changed the way it does business in relation to the detention, management and supervision of persons arrested at demonstrations and other similar events.

The Toronto Police Service now has a Mass Arrest policy that addresses the issue of supervision and accountability for the treatment of detained persons. Washroom facilities are now provided for the use of detained persons prior to transportation to a police station. Additionally, Court Services has written a Unit specific policy placing the onus for prisoner management and care on Court Services personnel in charge of prisoner transportation vehicles. These new measures directly address the issues raised by the public complainants and will, it is hoped, prevent a re-occurrence of the unacceptable situation encountered by them on October 16, 2001.

What occurred to the public complainants is not acceptable: it is not in line with the priorities of the Toronto Police Service. The Toronto Police Service acknowledges that management of these detained persons on October 16, 2001, could have and should have been addressed more adequately and it sincerely regrets that the complainants were detained in this manner.

The Toronto Police Service takes full responsibility for those events and offers its sincere apology to each of the complainants for the fact that they were treated in such a manner as to force them to endure unacceptable conditions on October 16, 2001.

As frightening as the story is, what the police force never did was apologize for the shoddy investigation that led to the complaints being "unsubstantiated."

It is fair to conclude that one aspect of police culture—protecting fellow officers—likely comes into play as police investigate alleged wrongdoing by fellow officers. In fact, it would be unusual if that aspect of police culture was suspended only in instances where some officers could state that their colleagues acted improperly.

In at least one instance, an officer has gone so far as to threaten those who complain in cases where the police investigating do not substantiate the complaint. Police officer Michael McCormack, a candidate to become president of the Toronto Police Association in 2005, suggested that if elected to the office he would enact a policy that the association would support an officer who sues anyone who files a complaint that is withdrawn or found to be false.

McCormack, son of a former chief of Toronto police, was not elected in 2005, but he did become president of the association in 2009. Given a change in Ontario law between 2005 and 2009, he is now probably unable to threaten complainants in this fashion. Nevertheless, given the power of police officers, many individuals fear retaliation by the police if they complain, just as they (rightly) lack trust in the effectiveness of a complaints system that the police control.

The situation is even more critical when the extraordinary power available to a police officer is taken into account. Officers are authorized to make arrests and to use force, and armed with batons, tasers, and guns, they have the means to do so at a moment's notice. Without an independent system for resolving a citizen complaint, there is little opportunity for public satisfaction with respect to any allegation of police wrongdoing.

There have been many calls for independent investigations, but they have been answered only in Ontario and to a lesser extent in British Columbia and Alberta. Ontario did possess a Public Complaints Commission that provided independent investigation from 1981 to 1995, when it was abolished by Premier Mike Harris. When Dalton McGuinty became premier in 2003, he took the opportunity to distance himself from the Harris years by appointing in 2004 the well-respected former chief justice of the Ontario Superior Court Patrick LeSage to propose a public complaints system seen to be fair, effective, and transparent, invoking the confidence of the public and the respect of the police.

LeSage recommended that an independent civilian body be established, with responsibility for the police complaints system in Ontario. This body would educate the public about the complaints system, receive complaints, assist complainants in filing complaints, and process the complaints. He recommended as well that complaints be filed by anyone, including friends and third parties; under the Harris regime, bystanders, witnesses, and third parties were not allowed to file complaints, putting the full weight of the process on those who had already suffered at the hands of the police. LeSage proposed that complaints could be made about policy issues as well as police conduct. He recommended that reports on the investigation be made available to the complainant, and that processing the complaints be done in a transparent manner so the complainant would understand exactly how the complaint was handled. Any police officer who harassed or intimidated a complainant would be deemed to have engaged in misconduct and would be appropriately charged.

LeSage put emphasis on the informal resolution of complaints by mediation, providing the parties agreed. Where informal resolution was not proceeded with, the complaint would be investigated under the auspices of the complaints body—that is, in most cases the investigation would be done by the police, with full reporting to the complaints body, and only in the most serious cases would the investigation be done by the independent civilian body itself. Where one of the parties remained unhappy with the outcome, a public hearing would be conducted before independent, trained adjudicators. The issue of penalties against officers would be left to the chief of police of the force involved, but officers would find that the penalty followed them if they sought employment with another force. Appeals from decisions, whether informal or formal, would continue to go to the Ontario Civilian Commission on Police Services and from there to the Divisional Court. Police boards would be required to order independent and public audits of the way they handle complaints every two years. LeSage also proposed that to ensure police can be easily identified for the purpose of complaints, officers would be required to be identified "by way of a significantly large name patch on their uniforms."

The provincial government introduced legislation in 2006 to adopt many of the LeSage recommendations, and that legislation was passed in 2007, establishing the Office of Independent Police Review Director (OIPRD). The office was finally opened for public use in October 2009.

Progressive as this legislation is, its shortcomings are worth noting. First, the way the legislation and the OIPRD are structured, many investigations will remain in the hands of the police, even though they are overseen by the OIPRD. Given the history of self-investigation, it has been argued that all investigations should be done by independent individuals. LeSage took the position that investigations by police would be fair if done under the auspices of the independent body, particularly if the independent body has investigators of its own who might intervene. He also thought this approach would create a sense of responsibility among the police for attending to their own misdemeanours.

Second is the issue of timing. Speed and early response are important to accurate investigations (evidence disappears quickly, and memories are awfully short), but it will not be until after the police have completed their investigation—perhaps taking two or three months—that the investigation will be reviewed by the OIPRD. After that time passes, if it is found that the investigation was not good enough, it may be difficult or impossible to do a reasonable investigation.

Third is the question of who the investigators are. Lesage suggested no more than half of the investigators on staff be former police officers, given the strength of the police culture and the tendency of officers to protect their colleagues. The legislation is silent about the percentage of OIPRD investigators who are *former* police officers. There is a fear that if most of the investigators used by the OIPRD in the few investigations it undertakes on its own are police officers, those investigations may not be as independent as a reasonable observer would wish.

At the time of writing, the OIPRD has only been open a few months. Whether these concerns have any basis in the real world will only be seen after the OIPRD has been in operation for the best part of a year.

British Columbia has begun to move away from a police force investigating complaints against its members. In September 2009 legislation was introduced to strengthen the Office of the Police Complaint Commissioner (OPCC), a provincial body. The OPCC will oversee (but not conduct) the investigation of serious complaints involving serious injury or death, and will determine whether the complaint may be investigated internally by a police force, or by an outside police force. Officers will be required to co-operate with the OPCC, including providing evidence. Complainants will be able to receive a copy of the investigation report, and to reply to it. The OPCC will also be able to deal with interjurisdictional issues, since the RCMP provides, under contract, policing services to some municipalities in British Columbia. These changes make the complaints regime in British Columbia similar to that in Alberta and Quebec.

The reluctance to establish an independent mechanism for investigations seems to flow from the understanding that police officers will refuse to co-operate with investigators who are entirely at arm's length, and that police associations and unions will vigorously challenge independent bodies. Police organizations express the view that outsiders do not fully understand the pressures police officers face.

In Ontario there is another body that reviews police actions, the Special Investigations Unit. The SIU is an independent body appointed and funded by the provincial government, and it investigates any police incident involving death, serious injury, or sexual assault. It has a staff of close to sixty persons, many of whom are located in the Toronto area. It responds immediately when an event occurs, often arriving at the scene within two hours of being called. In the fiscal year 2003–04, for example, the SIU investigated 192 incidents and laid a total of two criminal charges.

The SIU has been subject to much public scrutiny. The most recent report, "Oversight Unseen," by the Ontario ombudsman in 2009, was the seventh provincial report on the SIU in the past sixteen years. The report makes many recommendations on reconstructing the SIU into a strong, functioning organization, but its most telling comments relate to the hostility the organization faces from the police. It states, "Delays in police providing [to the SIU] notice of incidents, in disclosing notes, and in submitting to interviews are endemic." It also states, "Police interviews [by the SIU] are rarely held within the regulatory time frames and are all too often postponed for weeks, sometimes for months." Early in 2010 it was revealed that an incident from 2006 when a Toronto officer injured a civilian, was never reported to the SIU, as required by law. It is unclear how many such cases go unreported. Judge Wood's comment about the difficulty police officers have in relating to civilian authority are worth remembering. Several other provinces have expressed interest in establishing a special investigations unit similar to that in Ontario.

One other body in Ontario needs to be mentioned, the Ontario Civilian Police Commission (OCPC), formerly the Ontario Civilian Commission on Policing (OCCOPS). OCPC is a provincially appointed and funded body with a wide mandate to oversee municipal policing. Its duties include dealing with appeals of police disciplinary penalties; disputes between municipal councils and police service boards involving budget matters; the amalgamation of police services between municipalities; the conduct of chiefs of police, police officers, and members of police service boards; and reviewing the disposition of complaints against the police (as seen with the complaints filed by the teenagers in Toronto after the demonstration in 2001). Most of its work concerns the first item, namely, dealing with appeals by police officers to the way they were disciplined. Its role in respect to the appeal of complaints has typically not been large.

8

POLICE GOVERNANCE

GOVERNMENT EMPLOYEES ARE ULTIMATELY OVERSEEN BY THOSE ELECTED TO public office. Employees are managed by executive directors or deputy ministers who, like the organization as a whole, are responsible to a minister who is part of the government, or to a municipal council. Police officers, in theory, are no different. They are managed by a police chief who, in turn, like the police force, is governed by a body responsible to elected officials.

The most common arrangement in almost all Canadian cities is for the police governing body to be a police board rather than the elected politicians themselves. In Quebec outside Montreal, there are no police boards, and police report directly to provincial officials and local authorities, as they do in smaller centres in several Maritime provinces and in Manitoba. The RCMP, the Ontario Provincial Police, and the Sûreté du Québec do not report to a police board, but each reports to a cabinet member of the government involved.

Police boards are responsible for hiring a police chief, establishing a budget, creating rules and regulations, collective bargaining, and all the other responsibilities necessary to support the key manager, the chief.

Boards consist of three, five, or occasionally seven individuals specified by provincial legislation to be members (a mayor, councillors, or municipal or provincial appointees). Generally, provincial legislation states that smaller communities will have boards of three members, larger ones five members, and the biggest cities seven members.

One function of a police board is to provide distance between the police force and the political process, something not seen in United States, where a newly elected mayor usually appoints a new chief of police. On some Canadian police boards, elected representatives form a majority, on others they are in a minority. Most boards include at least one person appointed by the provincial government.

But there are complicated issues about police boards and how they function. One view was voiced by Prime Minister Pierre Trudeau in 1977, commenting on the RCMP: "The policy of this government … has been that … the politicians who happen to form the government … should be kept in ignorance of the day to day operation of the police force and even the security force … That is our opinion. It is not one of pleading ignorance to defend the government. It is one of keeping the government's nose out of the operation of the police force at whatever level of government. On the criminal law side, the protections we have against abuse are not with the government, they are with the courts."

A different view was voiced by the lawyer K.C. Palmer in his 1979 study of police governance in the Waterloo Region: "The arguments for 'keeping politics out of police' are largely fraudulent. No matter how the system is structured, the police governing body must ultimately be responsible to the public—that is accountability and that is politics."

The situation is made more complicated in Ontario, and by practice in the rest of the country, by a provision in Section 31 of the *Police Services Act*, which outlines the duties of a police services board. A subsection states, "The board shall not direct the chief of police with respect to specific operational decisions or with respect to the day-to-day operation of the police force." Legislation making it clear that board members cannot tell the chief that a particular person should or should not be arrested, or that the police should take a certain approach to a problem is reasonable. Such intrusions would allow politicians to use the police against their enemies. But that has not been how the subsection has been interpreted. Instead, it has been interpreted to mean that the police board should have nothing to do with any operational policy. Thus, the Toronto Police Services Board has never been willing to take a strong position about strip searches and what seems to be an overuse of them in the face of the Supreme Court of Canada decision. The board has backed away because a policy about strip searches would be "operational" in nature. In taking this approach, police boards have divorced themselves from any active role in shaping how policing occurs in local communities.

The criminologist Clifford Shearing addressed this issue in his recommendations for restructuring the Northern Irish Constabulary in the late 1990s. He suggested a distinction should be made between operational independence and operational responsibility. He thought interference by politicians in day-to-day policing was wrong, but that oversight of operational matters was entirely legitimate. If there is to be any accountability, he said, there must be scrutiny of the operational domain. That is what a local municipal council does with respect to its staff: it does not intervene in the garbage collection or waste water treatment, but it does set policies regarding how those tasks will be delivered and performed. Why should the police be treated any differently?

The dictum of Lord Denning about police officers cited in Chapter 4 is a stumbling block to this kind of accountability: "No minister of the crown can tell [a police officer] that ... he must or must not prosecute this man or that one. Nor can any police authority tell him so. The responsibility of law enforcement lies on him. He is answerable to the law and the law alone." Surely making the officer an entirely free agent is not a responsible way to run a police force. It would assume there should be no controls on individual discretion, and that policing is something of an anarchic practice.

Thus, there is some question about the degree of accountability practiced by police boards in Canada. The accountability deficit is even more
apparent when considering the kinds of things police boards might do
to become accountable even with a stultified interpretation of Section
31. The list of actions that would usually be associated with an accountable body such as a good city council would include ensuring that the
public is informed on issues, and that information on the service is readily available; having a decision-making process that is transparent, open,
and accessible to the public; ensuring that there is full debate of various
options and alternatives; and creating a sense of public ownership of the
enterprise.

Sadly, there is not an example of a police board in the country that
practices these approaches. There seems to be resistance to talking about
how a police force operates, how productivity might be improved,
actions that could be taken to reduce crime, and so forth. Occasionally police chiefs hold public meetings where people say their piece, but
it is difficult to think of a single police board that helped bring public
focus to a policing issue and then encouraged vigorous public debate.
Furthermore, much police business is done in private, and not in the
public session of board meetings.

Admittedly, few decision-making bodies wish to draw attention to
themselves since that is bound to lead to criticism—perhaps one reason
why police boards do not take the lead in debate. Moreover, there are very
few organizations to be found in Canada that make it their job to stay on
top of police issues, which means there are few challenges to what police
boards do or don't do. Without being challenged, boards can feel comfortable in their general silence. But perhaps the most significant reason
why police boards do not provoke debate and criticism about policing
issues is the fear that members who criticize will be challenged by police
associations and unions. There is a worrying example from Edmonton.
In November 2004, Martin Ignasiak, chairman of the Edmonton police

commission, attended a Canadian Association of Journalists event at a local bar along with Kerry Diotte, an *Edmonton Sun* columnist. Police said they had received a tip that Diotte was a risk to drink and drive, so five officers staked out the bar, and two undercover officers were on the premises. Both Diotte and Ignasiak left in taxicabs.

The stakeout came to light when a newspaper reporter heard Diotte's name mentioned on the police scanner. Two weeks later Police Chief Fred Rayner launched an investigation into the sting operation, bringing in the Calgary Police Service to investigate rather than keeping it internal to the Edmonton force. The police commission asked to be kept informed, and Ignasiak stepped aside during the investigation.

In February 2005, two senior officers were charged with discreditable conduct, one for his handling of the tip that Diotte was a risk to drink and drive, the other for sending out a news release that implied Diotte and Ignasiak were intoxicated that night. Chief Rayner cleared the seven officers who were on the scene watching Diotte and Ignasiak of any wrongdoing, saying they were just doing their job, and watching a number of bars in the area. But he also said that the names of both Diotte and Ignasiak had been inappropriately run through the police computer several times before the November incident, and warnings were handed out to four officers.

Then, on February 6, the *Edmonton Journal* published transcripts of police radio calls from the night of the sting, and the officers were heard talking about where Diotte lives, how excited they would be to arrest him, and the quality of his newspaper columns. One officer said that whoever arrests Diotte "will never have to pay for a drink as long as he lives." Another officer said he was getting sexually aroused at the prospect of arresting him. Chief Rayner then issued a statement saying he "strongly disagrees with the language and conversations on these tapes" and that "there is no question the eagerness these officers demonstrated at the prospect of charging him with impaired driving was clearly inappropriate."

On February 8 the police commission fired Rayner in a closed-door meeting. The next day, more than a hundred Edmonton police officers cheered, chanted, and applauded Rayner, who said he was disappointed by the action taken by the Edmonton Police Commission. Staff Sgt. Peter Ratcliff, head of the Edmonton Police Association, said, "I think this is a hatchet job, quite frankly."

Toronto is a hotbed of police intrusions on board members. During the past fifteen years there have been a number of examples affecting those seen to ask questions of police or be critical of certain policing policies. Susan Eng, chair of the Toronto Police Services Board in the 1990s, had her phone tapped—without authorization—by the police force, which, when challenged, said it was concerned about a lawyer who was her friend. (The lawyer had never been charged with anything.) The Toronto Police Association hired a private detective to follow Councillor Judy Sgro, a member of the board, and surveillance was obvious enough to her that Sgro felt intimidated and finally resigned from the board. City Councillor Olivia Chow found herself so often attacked by the police association that she too resigned from the board. Alan Heisey was chair of the board, and was accused of making remarks that a police officer interpreted as favouring the sexual exploitation of children. A reputable former judge was asked to investigate and found the allegations were completely without merit. Heisey served his term and then refused to put his name up for reappointment. Councillor John Filion alleged that police officers leaked personal information about him to the media, and did not stand for board reappointment. In Toronto, board members are in the invidious position of either kowtowing to the police force or being subject to nefarious pressures from the police. It is very unsavoury. Again, Judge Josiah Wood's statement about "the lack of complete acceptance by the police of the concept of full civilian oversight" comes to mind.

It is fair to say that most board members will feel cowed by the power of police. If police reported directly to a committee of city councillors rather than to a police board or commission, it is hard to see how the intimidation factor would be alleviated. Perhaps a larger board would be useful. If a police board consisted of a dozen or more individuals, debate would not be so personalized, opportunities for wider representation of groups and communities would be possible, and a feeling of greater public accessibility would be encouraged. Such innovations might help to reduce intimidation, as the power of numbers often does.

Clifford Shearing has suggested different functions for a police board, and a changed objective that might improve governance. In his book *Policing for a New South Africa*, Shearing indicates that the focus should be policing, not just the public police. He thinks civil society is best understood as fractured, and consists of a number of communities based on geography and interests protected by numerous organizations, some public and some private. He says that policing is the product of a network of interrelated institutions operating at several levels, with assorted kinds of knowledge and resources, and many of the policing institutions are private rather than public in nature. Public police play an important role, just as do private police, and Shearing believes public police should find their functions defined more specifically than they currently are. As Shearing and four co-authors state in a jointly authored article, "'[P]rivate' policing has quite as many effects on various 'publics,' both within and outside its domain (i.e., on those whom it includes and those it excludes), as 'public' policing has on private citizens." Hard and fast distinctions between public and private policing do not make a lot of sense.

Shearing believes that if we accept his model of how society creates its own security through this multitudinous group of actors, it makes sense to have one civilian body overseeing all of them, both public and private. He calls this a "policing" board, and such a body was recommended by the Independent Commission on Policing in Northern Ireland. It would work to ensure that the various actors interrelated with one another to the public's mutual benefit, and would make decisions about the allocation of public money. For instance, it might decide that a private group or agency could deliver some services more cost effectively or better than the public police, so funds would be diverted from one to the other. In this way, those bodies involved in questions of order and security could be seen as a continuum, and the false distinctions between public and private would begin to subside.

A policing board structured to play such roles would have to be much broader in representation than current police boards if it hoped to represent the various communities it served. It would hold accountable all agencies involved in policing. The public police would no longer have a monopoly on public resources or on its policing funds, and the policing board would assist in integrating the public police into other social organizations and activities. Perhaps the intimidation factor that today seems so pervasive in police governance would disappear.

9

POLICE AND TECHNOLOGY

MANY PARTS OF SOCIETY SEEM READY FOR A TECHNOLOGY FIX TO SIMPLIFY A job that needs to be done at a fraction of the cost. Technology fixes often turn out to have unexpected consequences in the way police work is done, and rarely seem to result in significant cost savings. This chapter will look at some of the more important technology changes that affect policing in Canada.

RADIOS

Police radios came into general use in the 1930s and permitted head-quarters to broadcast information to police cars, and the cars to provide information back to headquarters. They were intended to allow police to nip crime in the bud but never had that result, though there have been other positive ones. As Richard Ericson notes, the radio "has had a defin-ite effect on the organization of patrol work, enabling mobile officers to receive requests for their presence on a perpetual basis. This in turn has affected the way police mobilize police." The radio then became mobile, so that an officer on foot patrol had a radio.

Certainly the radio connection permitted a fast response from officers in the field, but that was not always appreciated by officers who often felt they were simply puppets fulfilling the orders of the dispatcher. Before the advent of the mobile radio, an officer could avoid radio contact by getting out of the vehicle and saying he hadn't heard the call. Ericson found that officers considered only 6 per cent of the calls exciting, and generally responding to calls was found to be tedious. The real impact of the radio was to push the police into a service that saw its priority as responding to calls rather than undertaking intensive surveillance or creating strong community connections.

THE 911 SYSTEM

Since the 1970s, emergency 911 telephone systems have been established throughout virtually the whole country for the purpose of allowing instant access to police, fire, and ambulance service. Generally the call is to a central office to determine what kind of service should be dispatched to the emergency.

Unfortunately, 911 is now seen by most people as the general access to the police department, and the service is swamped by calls; citizens seem unacquainted with the existence of the regular local police phone number. Strangely, it is not unusual in a large city like Toronto to call 911 and then be put on hold until a staff person is free to answer. And, as already noted in Chapter 2, more than half the calls received by the police (almost all calls come in via 911) are considered of such low priority that no response is made to them; many others receive a response in due course, but certainly not a speedy one. Enhanced 911 systems now associate an address with the call in order to pinpoint the location of its origin, again on the understanding that response time is of the essence, which is often not the case.

POLICE CARS

Police cars came into use in the 1920s; because they could cover so much more turf than foot patrol or horses, money would be ideally saved on personnel, but that proved not to be true. They quickly had another effect: they isolated officers from street activity, an isolation that seems to have grown more pronounced, so many forces have re-established foot patrols in some neighbourhoods to regain the community connection. As already noted, instituting two-man cars during nighttime hours was intended to improve the safety of one officer alone in a vehicle, which it has not done, but it does offer companionship. Obviously, cars are needed to police low-density suburban communities where there is very little street life. Cars have also proven to be good places to locate police equipment, such as a computer, needed to assist the officer.

An unintended consequence of the police car is the police chase. An Ontario report prepared for the Ministry of the Solicitor General in 1999 (after several deaths resulting from police chases) showed the extent of the damage caused by chases. The report found that between 1991 and 1997 there were 10,421 chases in the province (obviously, not all were on city streets) in which 33 people were killed and 2,415 injured, including police officers and bystanders, which meant that about a quarter of all police chases resulted in physical injury or death. Less than 2 per cent of the chases began because of suspected crimes of violence; one-third began because of a suspicion that stolen goods (including cars) were involved, and a further third because of traffic offences. More than 80 per cent of chases involved males under thirty-five years of age.

Most chases last for less than a minute, though some can go on for considerably longer. For his book *Blink: The Power of Thinking Without Thinking*, the journalist Malcolm Gladwell looked at influences on quick decision making and related that to policing. He found that a heartbeat rate between 115 and 145 (the normal heartbeat is about 70 a minute) can result in extraordinarily good decisions by an expert, and the increased rate might lead to very fine performances by athletes. But above 145 beats a minute, "complex motor skills start to break down … Behaviour becomes inappropriately aggressive."

Apparently that is what happens in high-speed police chases. Gladwell quotes a former Los Angeles police officer about driving through neigh-bourhoods at high speed. "Even if it is only fifty miles an hour. Your adrenaline and heart start pumping like crazy. It's almost like a runner's high. It's a very euphoric thing. You lose perspective. You get wrapped up in the chase ... If you've ever listened to a tape of an officer broadcasting in the midst of a pursuit you hear it in the voice. They almost yell. For new officers, there's almost hysteria." Gladwell notes, "This is precisely the reason that many police departments in recent years have banned high-speed chases."

Provincial governments have moved to control chases, mostly through the way they are authorized and conducted. In Ontario, Regu-lation 546/99 (under the *Police Services Act*) was passed to govern how chases must be conducted. It states that the officer must determine that "there are no alternatives available" and whether the chase "outweighs the risk to public safety;" the officer must notify the dispatcher, who then takes control of decision making. Such restrictions seem reason-able in a normal situation, but chases are anything but normal. The offi-cers involved are usually in a state of high excitement, with adrenaline flowing; the speeds are often very fast on streets where speed is usually restricted; and the chase is often brief. In these situations it is very diffi-cult to engage in objective decision making, which is what the regulation attempts to require.

Suggestions have been made that police chases not be permitted. If police begin to chase a car and the person pursued speeds up or tries to evade, perhaps the chase should be abandoned. Some suspects would escape, at least for the time being, but physical injury and property damage would be reduced. Chases may happen because they offer a little excitement in what for most police officers is a very tedious job.

COMPUTERS

One of the key tools for the police is the Canadian Police Information Centre (CPIC), a national computer database that most officers and patrol cars are linked into. It provides a great deal of information useful to the officer—criminal records, wanted vehicles, wanted people, stolen property, and more. When police stop someone and ask for a driver's licence, that information is often checked against the CPIC.

A more specific database is the Violent Crime Linkage Analysis System (ViCLAS), which provides information on and links to records of violent crimes and serial killers. Officers must fill out a detailed, structured questionnaire to use ViCLAS, and a crime analyst then looks for connections to other crime incidents in the hope of identifying a suspect. Computers are also used by some police forces for geographical profiling, which does crime mapping of locales to help identify a suspect, since most crimes are committed in relative proximity to a suspect's work or residence. Often psychological profiles of suspects are prepared, and they too are entered into the database to round out the picture.

Computers are used to check gun ownership, and therefore determine the risk that officers face before they arrive at an address. The information is available because of the federal gun registry, though the registry has been controversial since it was established, as mentioned, both because of its high cost (more than $1 billion to get it up and running) and because it requires the registry of rifles and long guns as well as handguns. Critics think that rifles used for hunting should not be registered. (As noted in Chapter 1, the number of people killed by rifles and long guns in Canada since the registry was established in 1995 has been cut in half.) Canadian police apparently access the gun registry more than six thousand times a day.

Apart from computers being a very useful information tool for police, various forces are experimenting with some of the social media such as Facebook to see how they might help with finding missing persons, gathering evidence and tips, or attracting new recruits. As well, large urban forces usually assign officers to search for computer-based child pornography.

GUNS AND THE USE OF FORCE

Possibly the most important piece of technology available to the police is the handgun issued to each officer. Given that it is rarely used—some officers, during the many years they serve, never fire their gun while on duty—the presence of the gun may be most important for its symbolism, namely, that police have at their disposal lethal force.

In a police context, gun use is considered within a use-of-force model, in which police are trained to use force appropriate to the situation. As proposed by the Ontario Police College, the model is described as circular, in the centre of which is the situation where the officer shifts from assessing to planning to acting. The suspect is judged to be compliant, passive resistant, active resistant, assaultive, or likely to cause serious bodily harm or death to himself or others. The officer's actions can escalate from simply being present, to tactical communication, empty-hand techniques, use of soft-impact weapons, use of aerosol spray, use of hard-impact weapons, and finally use of a gun. This use-of-force model makes perfect sense to the armchair critic, but as with police chases, things happen so quickly in real life that often there is little opportunity for on officer's reflection on the options. In virtually every case where an officer pulls a gun and uses it, the officer describes a tense situation in which no alternative seemed possible. Seen in retrospect, practically all their accounts of incidents suggest that outcomes would have been different (and less violent) if the officer had chosen a less confrontational option a few minutes before the shooting occurred. The problem is not so much about use-of-force as about police discretion, and, as already noted, discretion, a truly essential part of an officer's arsenal, is not part of recruit training.

Most police forces require officers to complete a report every time a gun is removed from the holster. When guns are fired, causing injury or death, an inquiry is undertaken, whether by the police themselves, the Special Investigation Unit in Ontario, or, after public pressure, through a public inquiry. It is most unusual for any such review to conclude that the police officer was at fault. One reason is that often the only other witness to the event was the individual who was shot, and/or other police officers, so the "other side of the story" is rarely heard in a forceful manner. (In some cases, officers claim a suspect had what looked like a gun, later found to be a plastic replica. Some critics have alleged replicas are left on the scene by officers, after incidents have occurred, as a way of explaining what happened.)

In the United Kingdom, front-line officers on patrol are rarely equipped with a gun, and some argue that police officers in Canadian cities should generally not be armed. Officers would be less likely to be shot, the argument goes, since it would be known they were unarmed, and members of the public would be safer as well. Guns could be left in the hands of well-trained back-up officers called to a scene; experience shows that highly skilled officers in an emergency task force or a hostage-taking squad have been trained to be calm in very trying circumstances and to shoot only as the last resort. The opposing argument, which seems to have carried the day, is that no Canadian police force has been willing to be the first to try the experiment of giving up their guns.

TASERS

A taser (an electronic stun gun) fires two barbed probes attached to the gun by seven-metre-long wires. On contact, a high-voltage, low-amperage electrical charge disables the victim for about ten seconds, allowing the police to seize that person. The taser manufacturer claims there is no lasting impact from its massive shock to the nervous system, though there are very few independent studies on health impact. Tasers were introduced into Canadian police forces early in 2000, but they had been used by most American police forces for almost a decade beforehand. A number of deaths have been reported after individuals have been tasered—several hundred in United States, several dozen in Canada, until the end of 2009. The manufacturer has strongly denied that the deaths had anything to do with the taser use.

Police have vigorously argued that the use of tasers would result in fewer shootings by officers, fewer and less severe injuries to subjects and officers, reduced public complaints and civilian liability claims, improved officer morale, and an improved image for the police. The benefits would flow, according to the police, because tasers would be used instead of guns in difficult situations. But it seems that the taser has rarely been used by an officer for defensive purposes: if the officer feels in danger, he or she will certainly use the best weapon available, and that is the gun. Tasers, it seems, are used mostly to gain compliance from a subject.

Perhaps the most infamous Canadian taser incident occurred in the Vancouver International Airport on October 14, 2007. Robert Dziekanski had arrived at the airport after a flight from Poland to meet his mother. He spoke only Polish and had not been on an airplane before. After landing in Vancouver, he wandered around the airport for more than ten hours, lost. Airport officials apparently made no attempt to find a Polish speaker to communicate with him. He became distraught, rearranged some furniture, but apparently did nothing of great violence. The last ten minutes of his life were captured on videotape by a visitor to the airport. It showed him somewhat confused, but not dangerous to other travellers who attempted to communicate with him and calm him. Then four Mounties entered the airport, and without further ado—Dziekanski was not objecting to their approaching him, and they were not asking him any questions—they simply tasered him. As he fell to the floor screaming in pain, he was tasered again and pronounced dead shortly after two of the RCMP officers had kneeled on his neck and other parts of his body.

The chain of events that followed captures something of the disarray into which a police force can fall after making such a serious mistake. The RCMP seized the videotape and refused to release it until the owner initiated legal action to have it returned. The video was then posted on the Internet, where it was seen by many people. The RCMP's early pronouncements to the media following the incident, in which the police described what happened, were shown by the video recording to be inaccurate in several important aspects. The RCMP commissioner, William Elliott, remained silent for more than a month, and then issued a written press release expressing condolences to the family, saying the officers had been reassigned, and that the taser is "an effective law enforcement tool." The RCMP refused to provide the names of the officers who confronted Dziekanski and allowed the officers to remain "on duty" for more than a month. Only after a public outcry were they reassigned to other duties. The Canadian Border Services Agency refused to say anything about its employees' involvement, even though Dziekanski had been under their watch for more than ten hours. The Vancouver Airport Authority was able to provide no satisfactory explanation for why airport staff was so unresponsive to Dziekanski's mother, who was waiting for her son, inquiring about where he was, and pleading for their assistance in finding out why he had not appeared at the doors where travellers exit from flights.

In late November, the provincial government finally announced the establishment of an independent public inquiry led by former judge Thomas Braidwood. Reporters with Canadian Press dug into the RCMP's use of tasers, and found that in the previous five years, 79 per cent of taser use was to seek compliance from a person when there was no evidence that the victim was proving violent or difficult to arrest. It was also reported that the RCMP used tasers with some frequency when intervening in domestic disputes.

Testimony at the inquiry proved fascinating, as RCMP officers made statements that seemed at odds with what the video showed. There were reasons to conclude that they had colluded before they arrived in this part of the airport to present the stories they would tell about what had occurred, and about their own actions. A report was issued in August 2009, and Mr. Justice Braidwood made some general conclusions as well as many recommendations.

One set of conclusions pertained to the condition of a person who has been tasered, one often categorized by police and by the Ontario coroner as "excited delirium." The term was used as though it was a recognized psychological condition (it is not) to describe a person who ultimately dies after being tasered. The judge said, "It is not helpful to blame resulting deaths on 'excited delirium,' since this conveniently avoids having to examine the underlying medical condition or conditions that actually caused death, let alone examining whether use of the conducted energy weapon and/or subsequent measures to physically restrain the subject contributed to those causes of death." Braidwood went on to say what he thought was a more appropriate course of action than using a taser:

> *The unanimous view of mental health presenters was that the best practice is to de-escalate the agitation, which can best be achieved through the application of recognized crisis intervention techniques. Conversely, the worst possible response is to aggravate or escalate the crisis, such as by deploying a conducted energy weapon and/or using force to physically restrain the subject. It is accepted that there may be some extreme circumstances, however rare, when crisis intervention techniques will not be effective in de-escalating the crisis. But even then, there are steps that officers can take to mitigate the risk of deployment.*

On the use of the taser itself, the inquiry recommended that police "be authorized to deploy a conducted energy weapon only in relation to enforcement of a federal criminal law," and that it only be used if the subject is causing bodily harm or the officer believes the subject's behaviour will imminently cause bodily harm, and crisis intervention techniques have not or will not be effective.

The data indicate that the taser is used overwhelmingly to subdue a person and gain compliance, not to protect an officer from imminent attack. In a report on local taser use in 2006, the Toronto chief of police noted that it was pulled out 156 times—often just showing the suspect the taser is enough to gain compliance—and of those cases, 147 involved individuals deemed to be mentally ill or otherwise disturbed. (Taser use is relatively low in Toronto and the rest of Ontario since the provincial government has passed a regulation stating the taser is a controlled weapon and officers may not be armed with one except in special circumstances. In the RCMP and in other police forces, a larger number of officers are armed with tasers.)

The Braidwood conclusions clearly speak to the use of tasers in situations involving mentally disturbed persons. Toronto police have responded with the establishment of Mobile Crisis Intervention Units (MCIUs) consisting of a team of a plainclothes officer and a mental-health nurse. The team attends any incident that seems to involve someone with a mental disturbance, and once there it begins a process of de-escalation and calming the subject. In cases where the MCIU has been present, there are no instances of taser use. The Toronto chief has reported that such units result in a cost saving to the force since the unit is able to have the person admitted into a hospital much more quickly than police alone could manage. It is a good example of finding a low-tech solution that is less expensive. In 2009 the Alberta government moved to institute such units into municipal police forces in the province.

VIDEO CAMERAS

The use of closed-circuit video cameras (CCTV) is becoming more prevalent. Many private businesses and landlords employ them, and there is no question that they provide useful evidence after an event has occurred. Police often canvass all property owners close to a crime scene to determine what material is on nearby cameras. Whether such cameras prevent shoplifting and other crimes is unclear.

Some police forces are now installing video cameras in high-traffic public areas, and in many cases engage in "live monitoring"—that is, they watch the cameras in real time rather than simply looking at tapes after the fact. Much debate has taken place about the impact of these cameras.

In 2009 in Toronto, claims by the police about their effectiveness were disputed. Professor Rosemary Gartner of the Centre of Criminology, University of Toronto, concluded that police data did not support a finding that calls for service had been reduced in areas where cameras were mounted, and in cases where there were reductions, she said they could not be distinguished from reductions that would occur by chance. She commented, "I would conclude there is no strong or consistent evidence that the presence of CCTV reduces calls for service."

Critical questions remain unanswered: do cameras reduce crime or diffuse and disperse crime? Are cameras effective only when there is real-time monitoring? What are the effects on a community's feeling of safety? Do cameras impose higher costs on police? Should police own the information they tape, or can others get it and use it as evidence?

Police are also experimenting with the use of video cameras to record their own work. Some forces sometimes use video during interrogation, to show that it was carried out without intimidation, and lawyers have suggested that all interrogations should be taped. Some forces are experimenting with videotapes in cars to show that their activities related to vehicles are not improper. The Toronto police force spent a considerable sum trying to find a camera that met its needs, but it was not until 2009 that its experiment with in-car videotaping actually began. (The Toronto force spent more than $8 million in 2006–07 to equip 140 cars. Entering any taxi or limousine in Toronto, a customer is routinely photographed by a video camera, so it's unclear why police needed so much money to do the same thing.) No final data are yet available, but the cars with cameras have been rumoured to have had much less interaction with members of the public than other cars. Some police forces now equip officers with body-worn video (BWV), such as a video camera on the ear. It has been suggested the device be used by Canadian police. The chief of police in Victoria tested such a device for four months in 2009, in consultation with the provincial privacy commissioner, and describes the benefits this way:

We have found that 87 per cent of officers who use the equipment felt that the quality of evidence they obtained was improved with the video; public hostility/aggressiveness decreased; public complaints were reduced to zero during the test period.

Cameras were not on all the time as this was never intended to be random police surveillance but a use of video to gather evidence in situations where we believe a crime was [being] or was about to be committed.

While we believe that BWV is here to stay, we are working through issues related to the costs associated with transcriptions and IT storage. The equipment has an instant playback feature you can show the accused "on the street" their actual behaviour—few then want to proceed to court. The BWV has a calming effect with many people.

The desire of the police to make more use of video cameras may be driven by the fact that video is readily available to members of the public who often tape questionable police behaviour with their own video cameras or smartphones. (Consider the Dziekanski case in the Vancouver airport, or that of teenager Said Jama Jama in Toronto in 2003, who, having been charged with assaulting police and hearing sworn testimony about how badly he had attacked an officer, was released after video evidence showed it was in fact the officer who had beaten the teenager. The officer was found guilty of assault and served a jail term.)

Another kind of video camera records the licence plates of cars parked on streets and compares them with plates from stolen cars. Apparently this is an easy and inexpensive way to discover stolen vehicles.

A distant relative of the video camera is the Mosquito, a device used by British police, which emits a noise that is very loud and disconcerting to those under twenty years of age but just a low rumble to those who are older, with less delicate ears. Like a video camera in a public place, it helps in dispersing youth.

PHOTO RADAR

Police have used photo radar to good effect, since the system provides an independent means to assess speed. Red-light photo cameras have had a more questionable impact, perhaps because they function without an operator: a camera takes a photo of a vehicle travelling through a red light, and a ticket is then sent to the owner. Red-light cameras are expensive, and effective for what they are asked to do, but it seems the public is not pleased about these eyes-in-the-sky trying to enforce the law.

HELICOPTERS

A number of police forces have helicopters available for regular patrol; most forces are able to secure temporary air support for specific functions, such as a natural disaster. Many arguments are made in favour of police forces controlling helicopters, like any other piece of equipment. Helicopters can provide rapid response, an easy view of a speeding vehicle or suspects, and views not possible on the ground. They also eliminate the need for high-speed chases. Arguments made against police helicopters focus on the expense (purchase costs are very high, as are operating costs if they are to be available 24/7) and the considerable noise they create in residential areas. Daily reporting from forces that have helicopters (such as York Region Police just outside Toronto) indicates that they seem to add little value to what officers on the ground are able to provide.

The key question for a police force is whether financially a helicopter is a priority. Most forces have decided it is not. Some have considered accepting private funds for the service, but private funding may be seen as an inappropriate way to deliver a public service.

In the United Kingdom, some police departments are equipping helicopters with halogen lights bright enough to cause visual discomfort to youths loitering and/or drinking in public places. Apparently this is an effective technique to force them to disperse.

PRIVATE ALARMS

One piece of technology that has an impact on policing is the private residential alarm system. Most alarm systems are monitored by security companies that automatically call police when an alarm is received, and a police car is sent out. About 97 per cent of alarms are false, and the cost of dispatching police on such calls is significant. Toronto police estimate that 2.5 officers spend about an hour responding to each alarm, and that in an average year that force responds to some twenty-three thousand alarms. Toronto and most other urban police forces now charge a fee for false alarms, in the range of $100 or more, so that the cost to police of responding to a false alarm is paid by the alarm owner, not by the public. Charges are passed directly on to the security company's clients, and some companies have found it more cost effective to hire their own staff to respond to alarms.

It would be fair to conclude that many of the technology fixes that the police have employed result from a confusion about the functions of police, the most appropriate responses, and the kinds of challenges they face. Having the police respond quickly to calls for service is not what's usually required, for instance, and perhaps the police should not be part of the 911 service. There are few good reasons to put the taser in the hands of anyone except a member of an emergency task force. Conducting general patrols in cars is a poor use of personnel and fuel whereas making information available through a computer hookup, by comparison, seems useful to daily police work. The benefit of real-time CCTV is questionable. The challenge before investing in new technology is to analyze police tasks realistically and determine how they might best be performed.

10

ORGANIZED CRIME

PEOPLE INTERESTED IN BREAKING THE LAW SOMETIMES ACT TOGETHER TO get what they want. Donald R. Cressey, an American criminologist and sociologist, in his book *Organized Crime and Criminal Organization*, lists five levels of skill and/or organization, summarized here:

1. Amateurs are two or more people doing simple deeds together such as robberies, break-ins, or muggings. These activities require no specialized skills and no planning to speak of.

2. Tacticians are those who engage in crimes that require some specialization (such as breaking a code or lock), and some tactics (such as selecting a target together). One example of criminal tacticians would be those who read obituaries in newspapers to determine when houses are likely to be empty so they can be robbed. Bank robbers are tactical criminals, one a driver, another a lookout, and so forth.

3. Strategists are criminals who have highly specialized talents that they use to plan significant criminal acts with others, usually in ways that do not involve violence. Strategists often try to operate without violence so the public doesn't feel under attack. Those engaged in stock market frauds fit into this category, as do those who devise Ponzi and pyramid schemes promising investors much larger returns than the regular banking system provides. The men who carried off the Great Train Robbery in the United Kingdom in 1963—a large-scale robbery that endangered no member of the public—were also strategists.

4. Corruptors are strategists, but they try to draw others into their criminal acts by offering a benefit. An example, on a small scale, might be bribing a building inspector or other person in a position with access to regulatory control that needs to be breached. On a larger scale, an example might be gathering a few like-minded people together to strip a company of its assets or running a drug operation such as those run by the Hell's Angels (though with their tough tactics, that group might fit into the enforcers category).

5. Enforcers are strategists, and often corruptors too, with someone in the organization whose job it is to ensure that a compromised person delivers what they want, even if it is through the use of force. The Fulton Fish Market in New York City was, until the late 1990s, controlled by a large crime organization that forced fish sellers to pay a protection fee. Enforcer and corrupter organizations can be highly dangerous, because violence is regarded as a means to do business. Youth gangs can fit the strategists, corrupters, and enforcers models. They seem to use considerable violence, perhaps through inexperience or perhaps to avenge a lack of status in society.

Corrupters and enforcers are often organized like a legitimate company with a corporate structure having clear reporting relationships. As we know from the business world, corporations can succeed because the structure provides a routine and predictable activities and responsibilities; as well, almost every person is replaceable, adding the need to play along to survive. One difference between criminal companies and others is the names of office holders, as is well known from the example of the Mafia: the CEO is called the boss or capo; a vice-president is a sotto capo; and below that are lieutenants, soldiers, and enforcers. A second difference is that the criminal organization usually shields the decision makers so that few orders can be directly traced to them. A third difference, particularly for the Mafia, is the rule of *omertà*, a sort of code of honour requiring silence: if a member is arrested and keeps silent, the organization will protect his family and provide them with an income. If he is not silent, his family might suffer.

Crime companies seem to engage in all kinds of activities, as they have for centuries. Pirates were well-organized criminals, as were the Canadian bootleggers making millions during the American Prohibition era in the first few decades of the twentieth century, as were those who smuggled Chinese persons into Canada during the latter years of the nineteenth century. Labour racketeering is one example often overlooked, with criminal elements controlling a union (the Teamsters suffered this fate for several decades in United States), who can then easily move into cargo thefts and stolen goods. Trafficking in women is controlled by crime companies in Eastern Europe and elsewhere. Gambling, prostitution, drug dealing, and loansharking continue to be commonplace criminal enterprises in Canada. Criminal Intelligence Service Canada estimates that there are almost a thousand organized crime groups in the country, most involved in drugs. About 175,000 cars are stolen here each year, one-quarter taken by crime companies. The Hell's Angels are presumed to be involved not only in drugs but also in strip clubs in Canada, finding women to work here and using the venues as drug distribution points.

An example of crime in the corporate world was provided by the Canadian financier Conrad Black and his colleague David Ratner. Working with several company directors, they took a personal cut when newspapers that were part of Black's corporate empire were sold. Payment was demanded for a "non-compete" agreement—that is, the buyer would pay Black a sum for his agreement not to set up a paper in competition with the buyer—which meant that millions of dollars went to Black rather than to improving the shareholder value of the company he headed. Black was found guilty of obstruction of justice and three counts of mail fraud in the United States, where prosecutors seem much more aggressive with white-collar crimes than in Canada.

Another example is Bre-X Minerals, a Canadian company that had its stock price soar when it said it had found gold in Indonesia. Questions were asked about the find, and only after the main staff person was pushed from or fell out of a helicopter was it learned that company personnel had "salted" the samples with gold. The president of Bre-X was charged with fraud but died before the trial. John Felderhof, a senior executive of Bre-X, was charged with insider trading, but he was acquitted.

There are many other examples. Alan Eagleson represented a number of National Hockey League players in the 1960s and 70s, and organized the Canada–Russia series in the 1970s. Along the way, he took a slice of the money and pensions that should have gone to the players. Carl Brewer, defenceman with the Toronto Maple Leafs was one of the few players willing to stand up to Eagleson, who was prosecuted in Boston, convicted, and spent time in jail. Once again, the Americans took the lead.

Garth Drabinsky was Canada's principal theatre mogul, but after a lengthy investigation he and his colleague, accountant Myron Gottleib, were charged in 2004 with cooking the books of his company, Livent Inc., by inflating profits and deflating costs, thereby bilking investors of hundreds of millions of dollars. They were prosecuted in Toronto, and in 2009 the two men were convicted of fraud and forgery charges.

Enron was an American energy company founded in the mid-1980s. It grew quickly by hiding its debt behind special purpose entities and financial tricks such as treating anticipated profits as real assets. In 2001 it began to collapse, and shareholder value of $11 billion fell to almost nothing in an eighteen-month period. Among others, its four most senior officials were charged with bank fraud, conspiracy, and other such crimes, and convicted: President Kenneth Lay, Chief Executive Officer Jeffrey Skilling, Chief Financial Officer Andrew Fasto, and Chief Accounting Officer Richard Causey. Their prosecution in United States was significant, but there was none in Canada, even though Canadian companies were involved in supporting Enron. CIBC, for instance, paid $2 billion in fines to American authorities because of its involvement in Enron.

And of course there are many examples, even in Canada, of businessmen offering high returns on questionable investments. The scheme goes well while the business gathers investors, since it pays high returns with the money that people think they are putting in as investment: when new investors prove difficult to find and sources of new money dry up, the scheme collapses and people discover their savings are lost.

More attractive to the simple-minded is the pyramid scheme, which unfolds when a sharpie claims that he has a revolutionary water pump (or some similar invention) that needs to be marketed. If an investor pays $2,000, that person will be allowed to market the pump. In turn, he or she is required to find three other people to join the plan, each of whom pays him or her. They will each need to attract another three, and so on. By the time it turns out that the pump doesn't exist, or it doesn't work, or whatever, the sharpie at the top of the scheme hopes to have amassed a fortune—there is little possibility that investors at the bottom will make money.

The economic impact of organized crime is considerable. In Italy, organized crime is estimated to represent about 7 per cent of the Gross National Product (GNP), and in Sicily it is estimated that 80 per cent of businesses pay protection money. In Quebec it was thought that in 1975 the cost of organized crime was the equivalent of 10 per cent of all taxes collected. In 2009, it was said organized crime had a stranglehold on municipal infrastructure contracts in the province, driving up their costs by about 20 per cent.

It might be large and visible, but organized crime turns out not to be easily controlled. A significant problem lies in the nature of the criminal justice system, which counts on the vast majority of the accused pleading guilty. Indeed, as already noted, police lay three or four charges for every incident to make a guilty plea the easiest way to resolution. When the accused demands a trial, it often proceeds with a judge and not a jury in order to reduce costs, usually an important factor for the accused. Those involved with crime organizations often have substantial funds and resources at their disposal, and they have no qualms about relying on the presumption of innocence. Their lawyers know the kinds of legal options open to them and every wrinkle that might be challenged. Trials end up being long and complicated, and in those situations mistakes can happen and evidence gets lost, allowing for appeals, which are sometimes successful. Some organized crime trials can go on for years or even a decade, during which time it is entirely possible the judge or one of the key lawyers might die or become incapacitated, in which case a new trial might be necessary as the process must start all over again. There are also questions about whether members of a crime organization are tried together (in order to consolidate evidence presentation), making proceedings even more complicated and prone to running into trouble.

There can also be problems in collecting evidence. Some crime organizations rely on the silence of their members. Hence, in Canada as well as in the United States prosecutors have tried to convict members of crime syndicates, such as the Mafia, for tax evasion. Some witnesses are murdered or simply disappear. (Indeed, organized crime in Sicily has few inhibitions about removing judges they are unable to control.) Police forces are not equipped to deal well with the collection or analysis of complex evidence, particularly of a financial kind, since they do not have the appropriate skills.

Furthermore, when individuals are tried together, it is not easy to prove they are related in the criminal activity in the way one would like, given the number of unspoken things that happen in arrangements in real life and the difficulty of finding evidence that individuals agreed to carry out criminal activities. To deal with this problem, the federal government passed legislation in the late 1990s targeting gangs by making participation in a criminal organization a Criminal Code offence. Among other things, the changes reverse burdens of proof about some elements of the organization's activities. It has not been clear that the changes have made prosecutions any less cumbersome. The Criminal Code seems to work best with guilty pleas. It is also very costly to build and staff the large courtrooms needed to try a number of persons at one time. And the security cost of protecting witnesses against violent gangs is very high.

Attempts to deal with the emergence of youth gangs armed with guns indicate the problems the police face in pursuing organized crime. In Toronto, police made sweeps, arresting many people: in the case of the Malvern Gang, a group of young men who dealt in drugs in north-east Scarborough, some sixty persons were arrested in 2004 and charged with drug offences, possession of guns, and crimes of violence; in other cases, the numbers were one-half or one-third of that. But many of those arrested could be charged with only minor crimes, and accordingly they were released on bail, while others found charges against them quickly dropped; both outcomes led to the perception that the police might have overreacted. Those charged with more serious crimes were subject to lengthy incarceration while awaiting trial, opening up the possibility of dismissal on the Charter of Rights and Freedoms ground that the trial did not take place in a timely fashion. Powerful arguments have been made that it would be much more effective for police to play a preventative role, rather than pursuing the good optics of large numbers of arrests.

Recognizing that policing is structured to deal mostly with street crime, and that officers rarely have the contacts or the skills to investigate highly organized crime, one can suggest three possible courses of action. First, specialized bodies, either public or private, could be given responsibility for investigating cases, and then instructed to turn the data over to the police for charges to be laid. The Investment Dealers Association currently performs this role with respect to stock market matters, but it finds relations with police are not always productive. Police assume that others do not understand their role, and they don't appreciate that others might try to do their work. Moreover, police don't understand stock market crimes, so even when they are given the data, few prosecutions follow.

A second possibility is to establish a body that can do its own investigation, lay charges, and undertake prosecution, without relying on the police. The Ontario Securities Commission has this function with regard to stock market crimes, but it has proven ineffective, taking on only one or two cases a year, and rarely bringing successful prosecutions. (It lost the case against the Bre-X official, referred to above.) The Ontario Securities Commission is a public body, so this is not an example of private policing but policing by a body other than a police force.

A third possibility is to create a special branch within a police force to deal with certain kinds of organized crime. The Integrated Market Enforcement Team (IMET) is such a body within the RCMP. It is limited by the fact that it is not seen as a priority within the RCMP, yet it is subject to all the RCMP's rules about how positions must be filled and how work must be tendered to obtain the best price for consultants, even for lawyers and other experts. It is also hobbled by Canadian laws of disclosure, which include disclosing to those accused where all the prosecution's information came from. Most international bodies (a number of American groups dealing with organized crime, for instance) are protected from such disclosures in their own countries, and in order not to reveal their sources they do not want to co-operate with Canadian authorities. In addition, Canadian law does not permit agencies such as IMET to compel accountants to testify under oath to force them to share whatever information they have. In contrast, American practice allows authorities to require witnesses to testify under oath. For these reasons, IMET is not seen as an effective means to fight organized crime in the financial sector. The American system of publicly electing prosecutors is also important, since they make names for themselves with successful prosecutions and that is an enticement in successful prosecutions.

Perhaps a further problem for Canada with respect to organized crime in financial areas is that there is no national securities commission, covering the whole country. Instead, the stock markets in Toronto, Montreal, and Vancouver operate independently under different authorities, and some investors are concerned enough about aspects of those markets that they do not invest here. In late 2009 the Minister of Finance for Canada, Jim Flaherty, suggested it was time to establish a national body, but that did not meet with a great deal of enthusiasm in either Montreal or Vancouver, where both markets seemed to feel they would lose power and status. In any case, a national securities body might show no more special prosecutorial skills than the Ontario Securities Commission.

An even more difficult form of organized crime for police to deal with is corruption within a force, when officers themselves form an organization to pursue criminal purposes. This kind of situation comes to light relatively rarely in Canada, but the examples that do occur show the police are somewhat reluctant to vigorously prosecute their own.

Two examples from Toronto are relevant. One involved John Schertzer of the drug squad, and five of his colleagues. Schertzer had been the subject of several internal investigations by the Toronto police in the 1990s, but nothing came of them. Finally, the allegations from Toronto lawyers grew loud enough that the RCMP was brought in to undertake a quasi-independent investigation into the claims that Schertzer and his colleagues were beating up drug dealers, then stealing their drugs and their money. Six officers were charged with various crimes in 2004. By 2006 the Crown attorney was troubled by the inability of the investigating squad to prepare evidence, so he wrote a scathing letter to the police authorities. A trial judge decided in 2008 that prosecution had been so tardy that the officers had been denied a fair trial, and the charges were dismissed. On appeal, the court decided the charges should proceed, but as of the time of writing—now more than six years after the charges were laid—the matter remains under appeal.

The other case involved allegations that several senior officers sought and received payoffs from local nightclub owners, and in return agreed the owners would not face many liquor licence violations and similar charges. Criminal charges were laid against four officers in 2004. Again, the cases were not prosecuted with any degree of alacrity, and when a judge dismissed them in late 2009 because they had not proceeded in a timely fashion, everyone agreed there was no reason to appeal. Thus, the allegations were never proven in court.

In both cases, the officers involved had the strong support of the Toronto Police Association, which paid all legal costs, so there was nothing standing in the way of the officers fighting the charges, and they did. Some wonder whether the solidarity of the police culture played any role in the delays that resulted in the trials not taking place.

It is fair to say that police forces do not have any significant impact on organized crime. As just one example, the police seize a very small part of the illegal drugs in circulation. Taking one person out of an organization, even if it is the leader, does not seem to inhibit the organization, which carries on. One suggestion is that the government legitimize activities that organized crime now controls, such as gambling and the distribution of marijuana and other drugs. But a response is that governments have already moved into gambling, and now derive large revenues from it, while organized crime has simply moved into other forms of gambling that are still illegal, such as betting on the outcome of sports games. The feeling persists that whatever government does, organized crime will always bring forward new products to provide revenue.

Some prosecutions in the United States have been effective against white-collar criminals, as already noted, and that can be attributed to independent (elected) prosecutors who are adequately funded to carry out their work. Making such changes in Canada is unlikely, given that we see prosecutors as part of a government bureaucracy and fund them accordingly, but in any case, the impact on organized crime would be no more significant than in the United States, where it is small. Perhaps the real story of organized crime in society is about the limits of public policing in a contemporary liberal state.

11

COMMUNITY POLICING AND CRIME PREVENTION

COMMUNITY POLICING IS THE PHRASE USED MOST OFTEN TO DESCRIBE A PRO-gressive approach to policing (David H. Bayley calls it "the strategic flavor of the decade"), but it has been applied to so many activities that its precise meaning has become strained and uncertain. The idea developed in the late 1970s and early 1980s, after studies were published showing that traditional policing was not as effective as it should be.

The Kansas City study on patrol work in the early 1970s seemed to indicate that increasing the number of patrols did not lead to an increase in arrests or in the general feeling of safety and security in the community. That study put in doubt the notion that police presence reduced crime. A major study about response times published in 1980 showed that quick response didn't have a significant impact on arrest rates or feelings of safety. Several studies about the same time concluded that most crime solving came from the public, not from detectives. In 1982, *Broken Windows* by James Q. Wilson and George Kelling was published, arguing that if police fixed the little things in a deteri-orated neighbourhood by charging people for the minor crimes they com-mitted, that would begin to address and reduce the larger crimes affecting the neighbourhood. It was an argument based on the notion that small crimes lead to larger crimes, so the best prevention technique is to tackle the small ones.

Added to changes in perception about police work and crime was the increased level of education in society from the early 1970s onwards, with larger numbers of youth graduating from high school and attending universities and community colleges. Police officers themselves were earning university degrees, and they expected to play a stronger role and have more status within police organizations. All these factors led to a search for a new way to look at policing. Some said that it wasn't new as much as a reiteration of the principles Sir Robert Peel expressed in 1829 with the establishment of the Metropolitan Police in London. Peel had famously asserted that "the police are the public and the public are the police; the police being only the members of the public who are paid to give full-time attention to duties which are incumbent on every citizen, in the interest of community welfare and existence."

A statement by the government of Alberta best expresses the intention:

> Community policing is a philosophy, an attitude and an organizational strategy that promotes a partnership between the people in the community and their police service. Together, as equal partners, the police and the community must work toward solving the neighbourhood problems related to crime, fear of crime, and social and physical disorder—looking beyond differences in improving the overall quality of life in the community.

The statement is accompanied by a photo of a smoking barbeque with the caption, "This is a crime-fighting barbeque." Toronto police chief Julian Fantino famously remarked in a disparaging tone, "Community policing is flipping burgers."

In the larger picture, there are three elements that community policing hoped to embrace. First, it would represent a police force with an expanded role in society because it would be proactive and not just responsive. Police would look for ways to address and resolve underlying problems, much as a community social worker does. Police would learn from the community about dangerous intersections and help amend traffic regulations; they would learn of iffy parts of local public space and help secure better lighting. They would advocate for more community parks and recreation programs and facilities.

Second, community policing implied organizational change in the police force, from a system based on military discipline and hierarchy to something flatter, with officers at the bottom having a larger say in the work undertaken and in the priorities. The officer wouldn't merely follow orders but could lend expertise and be involved in decision making. Third, community policing could promote better links between police and community, and regular interaction with community organizations and agencies. This change might lead to more foot patrols in appropriate neighbourhoods with pedestrian traffic and shopping strips.

One of the initial manifestations of community policing was the Neighbourhood Watch program beginning in the 1970s, with residents encouraged to confer with police about the need to pay attention to strangers and suspicious activity and to take precautions to prevent break-ins. The original idea was that community members would meet regularly to share concerns and ideas about how they could help police themselves. The legacy of the program—Neighbourhood Watch signs on lampposts in many cities across Canada—marks the fact that first meetings were held in many neighbourhoods, but little has happened since that time. The irony is that police were more likely to speak to communities strong enough to organize themselves well, but they were not the places that needed more policing: it was the weaker and poorer communities that needed assistance, but they were the most difficult to organize. It is reasonable to say that the Neighbourhood Watch program played no role in helping provide more secure communities or in reducing police work.

A related program was Crime Stoppers, which asked residents to make anonymous phone calls to report criminal activity. Many signs of the program continue to be seen across the country, though it is unclear the extent to which useful reporting occurs.

Team policing emerged from the community-policing ideas, and it proposed that instead of beat officers "turning over" the crimes they had discovered for other officers to prosecute and process, the team would take charge and deal with the case from start to finish, keeping the community involved. It was a good idea in principle, but it didn't fit within the existing police organizational model, and officers in a team feared they would be cut off from opportunities within the force. Furthermore, organizational lethargy meant that some persons were often loath to give up responsibilities that the team wanted. Team policing never became widely established.

Intelligence-led policing was another initiative: police decisions about where to place resources were to be based on an analysis of what kind of crime occurs in which locales. It is similar to "targeted policing:" crime data tells police which individuals or areas should be the focus of police action. This project might imply saturation policing of "hot spots" (where crime is known to occur) for a few weeks, or developing programs to concentrate on repeat offenders. Many police forces use these approaches, though only rarely in conjunction with community leaders.

Problem-oriented policing was based on the presumption that the police and the community would determine the nature of the problem that caused a lack of safety and security, then resolve it. It rarely proved viable. For instance, in the 1990s when crack cocaine came to Canadian cities, neighbourhood leaders often found it very difficult to secure police assistance in monitoring crack houses and laying charges. It seemed as though police were not much interested in taking action. Often it was learned that it was easier to convince the landlord to evict the offenders than to get the police to lay charges.

Yet another manifestation was the setting-up of community police stations, or satellite stations. The idea was that in a local station, perhaps in a trailer, the police would have more interaction with the community, but it has rarely proved useful. Local stations added little to police efficiency or community security, and often after a fanfare launch they were open only a limited time every week before being shut down as an ineffective way to spend public money.

Many police forces have established community-liaison committees, which can be regular forums where officers and community members meet to discuss concerns. The forums might involve members of certain community agencies as well as representatives of community groups. Like all such initiatives, success often depends on whoever happens to be at the table and the resources they are willing to bring to bear on the issues discussed. In some cities, the police have been wary of who is at the table, and do not permit organizations to choose their own representatives. (This has been the case in Toronto, and it has severely limited the effectiveness of some committees.)

Police divisions are often sites for officers to engage with youth in recreational activities of various kinds. Often seen as remedial programs, the significant benefit they provide is that officers get to know local youth on a personal basis, and that seems very helpful in reducing tensions between them. To that extent, these programs fit the model of community-based policing well.

The theories behind community policing have led to little significant change in the way policing services are delivered in Canada, for a number of reasons. The decentralization involved means that middle managers—police officers on the way up—lose whatever clout they think they should have under community policy models, and accordingly they are not enthusiastic about making the changes needed. Another pressure is the shift work that policing requires: an officer available on day shift one week would not be available again during days for another four or five weeks. Some officers feel community obligations make for a heavier workload. (Recreation programs, for instance, are not part of the work shift for officers.) And there are larger structural issues as well, such as the distancing from ordinary people that policing culture implies, the fact that police management is generally resistant to change, and the lack of clarity among the public about what the police should do to improve safety and security in the community. Few people want to attend a community meeting if there is no pressing problem to resolve.

The general intention of community policing is to reduce crime, and it can be expressed in a number of ways, only some under the control of the police. Crime prevention might be organized into four different approaches. One approach is to make it more difficult for crimes to be committed. Putting a very visible lock on a steering wheel decreases the chance a car will be stolen. Controlling building or room access by means of an entry phone or computer password restricts undesirables' entry to commit a crime. A gun registry makes it more difficult for someone to get a gun.

A second approach is to increase the risk of being caught. That's the thinking behind tagging clothes sold in shops, screening baggage at airports, and CCTV screening. Some urban designs are better than others in providing natural human surveillance through site lines and windows, or "eyes on the street."

Third, the potential reward of a criminal act can be reduced. If, for instance, property is clearly identified by registration or a licence plate, it is much easier to trace. This is the rationale for computer-program user agreements, which set out the rules for acceptable behaviour with a company's product.

Fourth, action can be taken to remove any excuse for stating that a crime was committed unknowingly. That's why governments require customs declarations forms to be filled out, and why speed limits are displayed on roadside signs.

Police obviously play very limited roles in the initiatives described here. They can encourage the public to adopt ways of preventing crime, but in most cases the effective action must be taken by someone else. As discussed in Chapter 2, effective action to improve safety and security is frequently taken by individuals and groups other than the police.

Here's a short list of what police forces often claim will reduce crime, followed by an independent analysis of the impact of each action:

- Increase the numbers of police officers, on the assumption that a larger number of officers results in less crime. Not proven.
- Increase random patrols, thereby reducing crime through greater police presence. Julian Fantino, former chief of police in Toronto and now OPP commissioner, states, "Police being visible on the street and in the community deters crime." Has been shown not to be true.
- Consider mandatory arrest of those accused of crime rather than releasing them, or releasing them without charges. Has not been shown to reduce crime.
- Increase community contact. Not proven to reduce crime.
- Increase contact with young people. No proof this is effective.
- Respond rapidly to calls. Has not been shown to reduce crime.
- Target those who have offended in the past. Has been shown to reduce crime, but putting offenders in jail also results in recidivism.
- Focus patrol on hot spots. Shown to probably reduce crime.
- Safeguard repeat victims on the assumption that protecting victims may prevent crime. Has been shown to be somewhat effective.
- Work more closely with social agencies. Has not been shown to reduce crime.
- Analyze crime patterns. May or may not reduce crime.
- Take a zero tolerance to any crime, even small ones (i.e., the broken windows approach). Has not been shown to reduce more serious criminal acts.
- Police proactively (i.e., using powers to stop, question, and, if warranted, search). Has not been shown to reduce crime.

More and more police forces seem to see the power to stop, question, and arrest as a crime prevention strategy, particularly when it is directed against young men. The New York City police force stops and questions about one million youths each year, and Canadian forces are following suit. Police have the right to ask anyone any question, but there is no obligation on the individual to respond. In real life, serious consequences ensue from not responding: police will take action, such as stating that the person is under arrest, or the person might be seized, with the threat of being taken to the station. Youths inevitably answer the questions they are asked, and consent to frisking. Their clothes and knapsacks are searched since they cannot afford to deny police requests—the consequences could quite possibly be assault and arrest. As was clear in Chapter 6 on racial profiling, police justify stops as a way to reduce crime and use the consent of youth as the basis for the frisking and searching, even though the consent might not have been freely given. Random stops certainly increase public resentment of the police, but they appear to do little to reduce crime.

The evidence is overwhelming that imposing harsh sentences, reducing the ability of judges to use their discretion in determining sentences, and putting people in jail for longer terms increases rather than reduces crime. Politicians who advocate such actions claim they are tough on crime, but they are in fact creating a society that is more dangerous, with more crime, and they impose higher costs on the public sector because of these outcomes.

The most effective way to reduce crime is through appropriate social interventions, particularly with programs and support directed at families and young children. Community workers actively working with and assisting socially disadvantaged pregnant women and mothers with children under two years of age is very effective at reducing youth crime. Working to improve parent management and peer relations of children in early and middle childhood are also very effective at reducing crime. It probably makes sense to take money out of policing and put it into proven social programs to meet a strong desire to reduce crime.

The criminologist David H. Bayley notes that more than half of the resources of any police force are involved in patrol and related activities, that detectives use another 15 per cent of resources on criminal investigation (with most crimes remaining unsolved), and he concludes that this work is really "dishonest law enforcement." They promise to prevent crime but don't. He suggests that if police agreed to get out of crime prevention, if they ended their monopoly, that would allow the public to do it, and do it well.

Bayley also throws out a number of other ideas for change. Maybe police should stop responding to calls for service, because few are emergencies, and few are crime related. Leave these calls to private security or to community service officers. Maybe random patrol should be abandoned (which is what fire departments have done). Perhaps detective work should be turned over to civilians, as happens in Europe or with white-collar crime in North America.

Bayley proposes an entirely different model for policing, one that seems to take the principles of community policing fairly seriously. He proposes re-establishing the neighbourhood police officer, one or two officers well known to everyone working in a small area as general practitioners. He believes that the community would get to "own" the officer, calls for service would decrease, and the officers could work with local residents to deal with hot spots. Supporting the neighbourhood police officers would be a full-service unit responsible for an area equivalent to a current police division. The objective would be to look at general police needs in the area and devise appropriate strategies to deal with them. Above the unit would be the police force, with all the support mechanisms needed—good managers, IT functions, money, infrastructure, and systems. Bayley hopes that in such a radically revised model, "thinking takes precedent over reaction." That indeed would represent serious change.

Bayley's proposals deserve serious consideration, and experiments should be established in several of Canada's larger cities. Logistically this would not be difficult. It would require looking carefully at several neighbourhoods in which to place neighbourhood officers for a year or two, and ensuring they had proper support from the rest of the force. In all likelihood no extra costs would be incurred, save the cost of a strong and independent monitoring system. One suspects the neighbourhood officers could forge strong and useful bonds with community leaders. If there is a difficulty with such an experiment, it lies with the lack of interest in police management in trying to do things in a different manner, as noted many times in this book.

12

OUTLINING AN AGENDA FOR CHANGE

How do we change public policing in Canada? Police forces are powerful, well funded, and rarely the subject of public discussion, except in instances of alleged wrongdoing. Then the debate typically focuses on assigning blame, but almost never elevates itself to the level of policy or how the police function in society.

As this book has tried to make clear, there are many issues in public policing that require attention, debate, and change. Police services eat up almost a quarter of the property tax revenues of many municipalities, and those governments find themselves under increasing financial pressure. Funds that could be used for youth programs, which have been shown to decrease crime, are instead poured into police forces that are unable to influence crime rates. It is rare that police spending is reviewed in order to increase efficiency. Relations between social service agencies and police forces need vast improvement. Police are probably the only government service that consistently treats people differently according to race, something that most people recognize is prohibited by law. Police functions are not well defined, and this absence of clarity often leads to decisions to expand the scope of public policing when restricting it might be wiser. The relationship between public and private policing is not always clear, even though private policing is growing because some people believe it is more effective in preventing crime. In short, there are many issues that deserve public attention and debate in order to improve the way public policing is delivered while ensuring the highest possible levels of safety and security in our society.

Yet any debate about policing is very difficult. Elected politicians are concerned that they will be seen as "soft on crime" if they are critical of the way police forces operate. Police culture is so entrenched that it often manages to destroy new initiatives. And police associations in the past have mounted attacks on those who recommend change or even limitations on police powers. Public figures who shy away from debate about public policing are simply being careful about personal consequences.

It is in light of these constraints that the following agenda for change and reform is proposed.

GOVERNANCE AND ACCOUNTABILITY

As Judge Josiah Wood stated, one key problem with police is their relationship to civilian accountability and to those charged with governing their activities. (He is quoted on this point in Chapter 7.) An extraordinary example of this problem was seen around the meeting of the leaders of the G20 countries in Toronto in late June 2010. Police activities before and during the event show the wide gap between what police do and the extent to which they are seen to be accountable.

Planning for the G20 took place over six or seven months. It was led by the so-called Integrated Security Unit headed by the RCMP, which included the Ontario Provincial Police and the Toronto police force. Officers from many other jurisdictions participated, as did a number of private security firms. A total of about ten thousand police officers were involved. The security operations (they also included the small meeting of G8 leaders in Huntsville, Ontario) cost more than $900 million, although it is unclear exactly how that money was spent—no public accounting had yet been made when this book went to press. By way of comparison, a meeting of the G20 in Pittsburgh in 2009 incurred police expenditure in the order of $30 million.

But it was not only the amount of money spent for the Canadian meetings that raised concerns: it was also the way the police conducted themselves. Upward of one thousand people were arrested in Toronto. Most were released without charge or with the very minor charge of disturbing the peace after being held for twenty-four or more hours in extraordinarily primitive conditions. Record-keeping of who was arrested and placed in the detention centre was chaotic, and lawyers were unable to contact their clients: police at the detention facility said they did not have the names of those arrested. Many of those arrested had been part of a large group of protesters and bystanders surrounded by police, police said they would be arrested unless they left, but they were unable to do so. Several hundred people (including young children) were trapped by police at a downtown intersection for four hours in a ferocious rain storm. Some of those arrested were simply passersby; others were journalists. Police, at random and without warrants, searched individuals on the street, in the subway, and on streetcars, even though they were a kilometre or two from the G20 meeting site or any demonstration.

On Saturday afternoon a small group of about fifty dressed in black with bandanas over their faces broke from the demonstrators and ran along main streets setting fire to police cars, breaking dozens of shop windows, and looting the windows of several electronics stores. The activity of this breakaway group was caught on the seventy or more closed-circuit cameras that police had installed at downtown intersections, but the police apparently made no effort to intervene to stop the property damage and vandalism.

Many questions remain. Who actually was in charge of police strategy, and how were decisions made? Why were large numbers of peaceful demonstrators surrounded and arrested? Why was there no police intervention to stop the breakaway group of vandals? Why were frightened shop owners who called police told that police would not respond to their calls, and that they were on their own? Who made the decision to abandon police cars so they could be set on fire? Who made the determination to conduct unlawful searches?

Such questions require answers from the responsible civilian authorities, but answers were not quickly forthcoming. By a vote of thirty-six to zero, Toronto City Council passed a motion to "commend the outstanding work" of Toronto police chief Bill Blair and his officers. Ontario premier Dalton McGuinty said the police "conducted themselves remarkably well." Federal justice minister Vic Toews said he thought the police did a very good job, a mark of which was that no one had been seriously injured.

Many citizens asked for an independent inquiry in order to get answers to these questions, answers that in any normal situation the civilian authority in charge would be obligated to bring forward. The RCMP reported to a federally appointed civilian commissioner, William Elliot, who did not seem to feel that his role was to ensure that police activities are fully transparent and explained to the public. The Ontario Provincial Police has a commissioner who at the time was a police officer, reporting to a cabinet minister. The chief of the Toronto police force reports to a seven-member police services board, but the board has indicated that many of these questions are outside its competence, since it does not deal with any "operational" questions. The civilian authorities over police showed little interest in responding to questions about how the police spent public money or why the police did what they did.

The example of the G20 is the governance issue writ large. There is no police board or civilian authority in the country that seems to feel its job is to represent the public interest in policing and that requires police to be fully accountable for all their actions in the way that employees who collect garbage, run the building department, or operate city parks are responsible for their actions. Police boards often seem to act as though they exist only to rubber stamp what the police force actually does.

As noted in Chapter 8, an accountable civilian authority governing police would ensure that: the public is informed on issues; information on the service is readily available; a decision-making process is in place that is transparent, open, and accessible to the public; there is full debate of various options and alternatives in police procedures; and there is a sense of public ownership of the policing enterprise. In practice, current police boards do not fulfill these mandates.

One change that may assist boards in achieving these objectives is to expand the governing structure in the expectation that by having more people around the table increases the opportunity for public debate. Most police boards consist of three or five members; Toronto's board has seven. If a police board was comprised of nine, eleven, or even fifteen members, there would be a much greater likelihood that public debate might be engaged as the individual participants discussed their differences. In some provinces legislation governs the size of police boards. To avoid the difficulties of rewriting legislation, boards might appoint large committees to consider and advise on policy questions; or local councils might appoint large safety and security committees to advise police boards. Size does matter: members of small boards fear that exposing differences is impolite, but that inhibition seems not to operate in larger groups, where debate is much more frequent. If debating police policy options could become a regular activity, new ideas would have a better chance of finding favour—as occurs with other municipal issues. Where police forces are governed by a single commissioner, whether a civilian or a police officer—such as the OPP or RCMP—a large police board of civilians should be appointed.

A second welcome change would be to slightly redefine "operational" so that, as described in Chapter 8, it does not include virtually everything a police force does. Clifford Shearing's idea that the civilian police authority should have oversight of operational matters but not of day-to-day activities makes good sense; indeed, in virtually all other governmental activities, day-to-day matters are the responsibility of managers with appropriate independence, but operational policies are subject to oversight. It is unlikely that new legislation would be required for this revised function—a simple variation in interpretation would suffice.

A third change would be for the major funder—such as the municipality served by the force—to be clear about expectations regarding how police boards should conduct themselves and issues that should be addressed in a given year. For instance, the municipal council could ask that the police board, as a matter of regular practice, post agendas in advance of meetings, permit public deputations on matters scheduled on the agenda as well as on those that members of the public wish to bring to the board; the council could also arrange two large public consultations on policing issues every year. And the council might suggest to the board issues that it feels should be addressed, such as racial profiling, strip searches, interactions with youth, and so forth.

COMPLAINTS

When something goes wrong in a police force, one of the first demands by the public is for a better complaints process. Often, however, the problem drawing public concern is systemic, and relates more to the way the force is managed or governed than it does to illicit or questionable actions of individual officers. The failure too often is with the civilian authority, and a reasonable complaints process can never substitute for an effective civilian authority.

Yet a functional complaints process is necessary to look into the errors of individuals or small groups that are bound to occur within any human organization. A good complaints process helps instill public confidence in the organization, since it provides a sense of justice and accountability.

As noted in Chapter 7, many police forces do not have a complaints system that the public considers acceptable. Politicians sometimes find they need to respond to particularly egregious police actions, and the means they turn to is a public inquiry, as occurred with the death of

Robert Dziekanski after he had been tasered by the RCMP at the Van-couver International Airport on October 14, 2007. In that case, Thomas R. Braidwood, a former British Columbia Supreme Court justice, was commissioner, and his inquiry's second and final report was released in June 2010. The report recounted instances of RCMP officers having made "deliberate misrepresentations" about the incident or having taken actions that were "unjustified." It went on to summarize the public mood at the time: "The unprofessional manner in which Constable Millington and Corporal Robinson dealt with Mr. Dziekanski, and all four officers' less-than-forthright accounting for their conduct, have had repercus-sions that extend far beyond this one incident. Mr. Dziekanski's death appears to have galvanized public antipathy for the [RCMP] Force and its members. That is regrettable, because the most important weapon in the arsenal of the police is public support. The tragic case is, at its heart, the story of shameful conduct by a few officers."

The report makes a number of recommendations to Canada Border Services and the Vancouver Airport Authority, as well as one key recom-mendation about public policing in British Columbia. It recommends that the attorney general of British Columbia establish an Independ-ent Investigation Office (IIO), similar to the Special Investigation Unit (SIU) in Ontario. The IIO would be mandated to investigate any police-related incident involving death or serious injury. It would be led by a civilian, and investigations would be conducted by civilians after a five-year setup period. The RCMP and local police forces would have no investigative authority unless authorized by the IIO. The incident scene would need to be secured pending the arrival of IIO staff; officers involved would be sequestered and may not communicate with each other; and witness officers (although not the respondent officer) would make themselves available for interviews by the IIO and turn over notes and other material to the IIO.

These are extremely useful recommendations, and the attorney general of British Columbia has stated that they will be implemented without delay. The central element is that investigations will be independent (not carried out by the police themselves), with a reasonable reporting structure, and the organization will have access to the funds it needs to do its work.

Similar organizations should be established to investigate all incidents of death or serious inquiry at the hands of police in Canada. Nevertheless, the experience in Ontario with the SIU casts doubt on the ultimate effectiveness of this mechanism. The safeguards proposed for British Columbia are, except for investigators' not being part of the policing community, all in place in the SIU. But officers do not always notify the SIU of incidents immediately; officers have challenged what kind of injury is considered "serious;" officers have refused to make themselves available for interviews until considerably after an incident; and officers have retained a common lawyer and thereby shared their stories. As noted in Chapter 7, the SIU has been subject to a number of inquiries in Ontario.

Excluding former police officers from investigative roles in the IIO gives the appearance of necessary distance. This exclusion was considered by Patrick LeSage in his report on a model for investigating complaints against the police in Ontario, but rejected. LeSage gave some weight to the argument that only other police officers understood the pressures the police were under, and thus they would not be willing to co-operate fully with investigators who did not have police experience.

In spite of its shortcomings, the Braidwood proposal should be endorsed and enacted throughout the country. It would improve the sense of accountability and provide more information to the public about police activities.

The IIO and the SIU are not established to deal with public complaints, although they do review incidents of death and serious injury that most likely would become the basis of complaints. Also needed is a body that can deal with complaints of any kind about police officers and police forces. As discussed in Chapter 7, the leading example of a public complaints mechanism in Canada is the Office of the Independent Police Review Director in Ontario. The benefits and limitations of the OIPRD are canvassed in that chapter, and it is noted that the short time in which the office has been operational means that it is not clear how well it works. Nevertheless, it is the model around which other jurisdictions in Canada should structure a complaints mechanism to ensure that it is independent and relatively transparent.

DEFINING REAL POLICE WORK

Job descriptions are important in setting expectations for employees and employers. Bad or inaccurate job descriptions create confusion of purpose and intent. The job description of the police officer defined by legislation across the country, as noted in Chapter 2, is way off base and defines police work as mainly concerned with crime, which represents but a small percentage of what police do. It is time that the job description be changed to reflect the real job done by police officers.

A good place to start is with the description of police duties as noted by Herman Goldstein in Chapter 2:

1. To prevent and control conduct widely recognized as threatening to life and property (serious crime).
2. To aid individuals who are in danger of physical harm, such as the victim of a criminal attack or automobile collision.
3. To protect constitutional guarantees such as the right of free speech and assembly.
4. To facilitate the movement of people and vehicles.
5. To assist those who cannot care for themselves, the intoxicated, the addicted, the mentally ill, the physically disabled, the old and the young.
6. To resolve conflict, whether it be between individuals, groups of individuals, or individuals and their government.
7. To identify problems that have the potential for becoming more

serious problems for the individual citizen, for the police, and for the community (crime prevention).

8. To create and maintain a feeling of security in the community.

It would be helpful for police boards to review this list and determine whether it fairly describes the work its officers do, making amendments and additions as appropriate. Once the job is fairly defined in its different facets, the board and senior police managers would then be able to better establish productivity and measures of job success, and make determinations about the allocation of funds between functions. Being clear about the real work undertaken would also help identify the kinds of skills needed by members of the force, the appropriate management structures, and the reasonable balance of uniformed officers and civilians.

RECRUITMENT, TRAINING, AND BETTER MANAGEMENT

The recruiting process for new officers throughout Canada is relatively standardized, and it aims to hire a person who is generally intelligent, well mannered, and in reasonable physical condition. It gives no special preference to candidates with areas of expertise that a police force might need, such as language skills, cultural awareness, or special social, technical, or management skills. It assumes that all new recruits are much the same, will go through the same standardized training and then begin by doing the same kind of work. These matters are all discussed in detail in Chapter 4.

Virtually no other organization in Canada hires new employees in this manner. If a bank had a practice of requiring that everyone start out as a teller and then work his or her way up, you would be reluctant to put your money there. If surgeons worked their way up from hospital orderlies, you might be especially anxious submitting to an operation. People are generally hired with the credentials and skills needed to actively contribute to and improve an organization. Job descriptions are prepared and candidates are assessed on the particular abilities they have to fill defined positions.

The same procedure should be followed for the police. It would allow a force to hire a range of talent and experience that would help bring contemporary policing to society. Civilians who work for police organizations are hired for their fit: why can't this also be the case for uniformed staff? Certainly, special training will always be required to make new hires into members of a police force, although it might not be the mind-numbing sort young recruits now go through. Different kinds of training to teach how police function should not be a significant challenge.

This type of hiring would be a big change for any police force, and experiments with it should take place slowly after careful thought. Several uniformed positions that require special skills, such as a person to handle police dogs or someone to deal with youth outreach, should be determined, job descriptions prepared, and the needed skills identified. Appropriate training programs should be prepared. The job should be posted widely, and after interviews, a selection should be made followed by training tailored to suit the successful candidate. Care must be taken to ensure that recruits are not isolated from other uniformed officers: every attempt should be made at successful integration.

A similar approach should also be used to find good management staff. Police forces desperately need better managers, and assuming that because a person starts as a recruit s/he can become a good manager is not a given. Defining one or two senior management positions in a police department and then looking outside the police family to find likely candidates might be the most significant change a police force could make. Since one characteristic of a good manager is that s/he makes employees feel good about coming in to work every day, it is entirely possible that such a person would quickly develop a following among the rank and file, even though s/he had no previous police experience.

These experiments in recruiting and training are ones that forces of various sizes should undertake.

RETHINKING POLICE WORK

Being much clearer about the real work police do was discussed above. Closely related to that is the opportunity for police forces to experiment with the ways they deliver services. Most large organizations spend 2, 3, or 4 per cent of gross expenditures on research and development, looking for new products, and new ways of doing old work. Police forces generally spend nothing on research and development. It would make sense if a sum of money were set aside for this important area of activity—just 2 per cent of the Toronto police budget would be an astounding $18 million a year. The experiments conducted might involve patrol, crime analysis, new approaches to management and discipline, team policing, relations with selected social agencies and schools, and ending car chases. There are many issues mentioned in this book that invite experimentation. Rank-and-file officers would surely have many of their own ideas to suggest from the day-to-day work they do.

The key to successful research and development is to establish the objectives in advance, to keep good records during the process, and to undertake an independent assessment of the results. Those responsible for policing are more likely to implement the results of successful experiments if police boards are responsible for monitoring them. Establishing research and development as a normal part of police activities would help promote discussion in a non-confrontational manner that could lead to change. When police boards are establishing annual budgets, they should require that the chief set aside a certain amount for these experiments, and then determine what the experiments would be and how they would be monitored.

Some experiments might focus on how police officers can better understand and be more integrated into the community in which they work. One experiment tried in Seattle involved placing uniformed officers in social service agencies for two weeks at a time so they could begin to learn the kinds of pressures low income residents are subject to. Officers might be required to take such a placement every five years—it would lead to greater empathy between two segments of society, and also improved personal relationships between officers and social workers.

Another experiment might be to take officers out of the role of crime fighter and put them into the role of creator of stronger social order (less law and more order, as Irvin Waller, professor of criminology at the University of Ottawa, titles his book). Currently, some officers on their own time playing basketball or another sport with local youth to find a new relationship that is more helpful for youth than a criminal justice model. This experiment would move such a role from the efforts of a volunteer into the regular stream of paid work.

The basis of the experiment would be to see if youth could be dissuaded from criminal acts and associations through friendship and advice rather than continuing to use a criminal justice model that is clearly not effective at keeping some youngsters out of the system. Officers would be assigned on a full-time basis on a consistent and regular shift (not one that changed every week) to a specific community or communities with the job of getting to know the people who live there, particularly the young men, since, as mentioned, 80 per cent of crime is caused by males under thirty. Getting to know youth takes time and patience and must be based on mutual trust and respect. Officers would have to be on a first-name basis with kids and would have to be seen as non-threatening. They would have to make it clear that they are there to be helpful. Given the hostility many people in low-income communities now have toward police, this change in attitude would be big, but it is not impossible.

Officers should offer youth advice and help protect them from arbitrary searches and arrest by other officers. The best advice is something like this: "Doing the kind of stuff you are doing will get you into a lot of trouble. I do not want to see you arrested, and I am not arresting you. But if you keep doing that, I won't have any choice. You've got to stop.

I'm willing to help you, and I'll make sure other police officers in this division don't cause you trouble, but you can't keep doing this."

That's the kind of advice police are said to have given fifty years ago, but even if they didn't, most adults know that the understanding they received as youths from adults after they did something stupid was often what was needed to set them on a more fruitful path to adulthood. The biggest threat that supportive adults used to give was "I'll tell your parents," which was often all it took to get kids to smarten up. It was a philosophy that said the goal of police wasn't to arrest kids but to help keep them on the level and get on with their lives. It's one based on that principle of more order, less law. It's manifested all the time in middle- and upper-class neighbourhoods but almost never in poorer communities. It can only work well if the officer actually knows the kid, and the kid knows the officer.

This kind of experiment might be very useful in some low-income neighbourhoods. Officers would have to be taken off regular shifts to be assigned to the work for six months or a year, and policing would have to be changed to ensure that the communities with these assigned officers were not subject to the standard random patrol. Strategies would have to be devised so "outside" officers who are not part of the experiment would not be intervening in the work of the assigned officers by arresting youth for minor crimes.

One of the great merits of experiments that stress community policing is that it reconceives the way that police relate to the people whom they are serving, and it demands much different skills. Both are welcome changes that help modify police culture and begin to integrate police with society in new ways.

BUDGETING

The cost of municipal policing is mostly covered by local property taxes, with some special but limited grants made available from provincial governments. Thus local politicians are well aware of how police expenditures influence the municipal budget.

But little restraint is exercised on police spending. Police often seem exempt from the budget guidelines established for other city services. The result is that police often receive budget increases when other city services are held at the previous year's outlay or receive even less than in the past. Not only is resentment about police spending fanned, but money that could go to programs known to reduce crime (such as recreation for youth) flows into a police department generally unable to reduce crime.

It is not unreasonable to propose that when general budget guidelines are established for city departments, those guidelines should also be applied to the police service: it should not be given a free pass, as it so often is. Strict expenditure limits on government services often lead to innovation, and there is no reason why that cannot occur in policing. British prime minister Margaret Thatcher made very deep spending cuts to public services in Britain in the 1980s that forced the police to reinvent themselves in ways that put them much more in touch with the communities they were policing. It is true that when the police have been told in the past to modify the size of requested increases, they have often threatened to cancel popular programs. In instances like these, it would be appropriate for politicians to hold firm and tell chiefs of police that if they want to cut popular programs, the decision is theirs—as are the consequences. There is no question that trying to hold the line financially will be seen by some as simply attacking the police, but sooner or later the decision must be made, and perhaps politicians should begin preparing themselves for the challenge.

CONFRONTING RACIAL PROFILING

Racial profiling seems to be a fact of life within Canadian police forces, as noted in Chapter 6, even though most senior police officials agree it should not be happening. Nothing stands in the way of Canadian police forces taking the same action as American police forces, as was so forcefully stated by the Kingston police chief William Closs in that chapter.

In some American cities, as we have seen, officers are required to fill out cards for everyone they interact with. The race of the person stopped is noted, as well as the other information gathered by the same kind of carding in Canadian cities. The information taken by each officer is analyzed, and if it is clear that the officer is stopping more than a representative sample of persons from any one race, the officer is spoken to by a manager, and techniques are discussed to change the way the officer does his or her job. Obviously, organizational strategies can be used as well as ones designed to lead individual officers to different behaviours. The point is to focus on the problem, which is the officers' behaviour. Officers unwilling to change should be let go.

The challenge is to find managers who will take racial profiling seriously enough to bring in useful techniques to make change. Too many senior police managers do not see racial profiling as a problem requiring action. Closs was an exception who proved the rule, and one can see what little support he had when he embarked on a course of action that quite likely could have led to useful change.

Canadian forces can learn well from their American counterparts how to bring racial profiling to an end.

CITIZEN ACTION

The benefit of citizen action should never be overlooked. The few citizen groups that have been established to monitor the police in the past two decades in Canada have usually concerned themselves with allegations of police misbehaviour and wrongdoing. These groups have usually lasted for only short periods of time, given the difficulty of looking into complaints, the lack of a forum for resolving complaints, and the fact that police officers see the groups as attacking its members and therefore as serious political enemies. Ideally, a citizen group should concern itself with police policies of all kinds, and not with complaints which it will be unable to resolve. It could appear before its local police board on a regular basis to put forward alternative points of view about how policing is delivered, thus enhancing public debate about important matters. It could raise issues at the police board if it felt those issues were not receiving enough public attention. The Toronto Police Accountability Coalition (www.tpac.ca) has played this role in Toronto for almost a decade. It has not dealt with complaints but has focused on policy issues—strip searches, police intervention with the mentally ill, budgets and expenditures, racial profiling, and many other issues.

IN CONCLUSION

What's suggested here is not an exhaustive list of reforms needed with respect to policing in Canada, but is intended to touch on some of the key issues where productive change seems most likely and achievable. Opportunities for focusing debate of police issues often arise quickly and unexpectedly, but each should be seen as a chance to begin the public discussion that is so needed to improve public policing in Canada.

NOTES

1. MAKING SENSE OF CRIME STATISTICS

Statistics on crime in Canada are best obtained from the Statistics Canada website, www.statcan.gc.ca; click on Crime and Justice. The publication *Juristat*, found in that section, is very helpful and is where most of the data in this chapter are from unless otherwise noted.

Data on child abductions and car accidents are found in "Child- and Youth-Friendly Land Use and Transportation Planning Guidelines for Manitoba," by Richard Gilbert and Catherine O'Brien, Centre for Sustainable Transportation, University of Winnipeg, September 2009.

Data on violent deaths are in Sewell, *Police: Urban Policing in Canada* (Toronto: James Lorimer & Company, 1985), 39–40.

Data on death by guns in various countries are from the Johns Hopkins Center for Gun Policy and Research, Baltimore, published in *The New York Review of Books*, January 2006.

For crime rates among young males, see Richard Wilkinson and Kate Pickett, *The Spirit Level: Why Greater Equality Makes Societies Stronger* (London: Bloomsberry Press, 2009), 132.

Richard V. Ericson's comments on the dark figure of crime are found in his *Making Crime: A Study of Detective Work* (Oxford and Woburn, Mass.: Butterworth-Heinemann, 1983), 8.

The quotation from James Q. Wilson is from his article "Thinking about Crime" in *The Atlantic*, September 1983: 88.

The quotations about inequality are from Wilkinson and Pickett, *The Spirit Level*, 133–56.

The article about Joe Arpaio is from *The New Yorker*, July 20, 2009, by William Finnegan.

2. POLICE WORK AND PRIVATE POLICING

For a good discussion of the stages of discretion, see K.C. Davis, *Discretionary Justice* (Baton Rouge: Louisiana State University, 1969).

Jane Jacobs's book on how and why dense and compact neighbourhoods are safer than low-density suburban neighbourhoods is *Death and Life of Great American Cities* (New York: Random House, 1961). A useful book on the salutary impact of social programs on crime is Bruce Kidd and Jim Phillips, eds., *Research on Community Safety* (Toronto: Centre for Criminology, University of Toronto, 2004.)

Regarding security, see Jennifer Wood and Clifford Shearing, *Imagining Security* (Cullompton, U.K.: Willan Publishing, 2007).

Data on private policing can be found on the Statistics Canada website.

A history of policing can be found in Sewell, *Police*, Chapter 1.

The argument for giving more value to private police at the expense of public police is in Mike Brogden and Clifford Shearing, *Policing for a New South Africa* (New York: Routledge, 1993). David H. Bayley makes similar arguments in his *Police for the Future* (New York: Oxford University Press, 1994).

The relationship of public and private police in several Canadian cities is recounted in Dennis Cooley, ed., *Re-imagining Policing in Canada* (Toronto: University of Toronto Press, 2005), Chapters 2 and 4.

3. MEASURING POLICE EFFICIENCY AND PRODUCTIVITY

Data on Toronto police response time are from the 2008 Environmental Scan, Toronto Police department. Data on the officers per population and the cost per capita in various Canadian cities are from the 2007 Environmental Scan of the Calgary Police force. Data relating to other countries are from Statistics Canada, as are the global costs of policing in Canada.

Richard V. Ericson's study of shift work is in *Reproducing Order: A Study of Police Patrol Work* (Toronto: University of Toronto Press, 1982). See also his *Making Crime: A Study of Detective Work* (Oxford and Woburn, Mass.: Butterworth-Heinemann, 1983).

Studies about how detectives resolve cases, and the failure of general patrol, are found in the collection of essays, *What Works in Policing,*

David H. Bayley, ed. (New York: Oxford University Press, 1997). The study about two-man cars is found in Sewell, *Police*, 228. The quotation about two-man cars is from Malcolm Gladwell, *Blink: The Power of Thinking Without Thinking* (New York: Little Brown, 2005), 234.

Shift information is available at http://911abc.com.

4. RECRUITMENT, TRAINING, AND MANAGEMENT

The Constable Selection System in Ontario can be found at www.mcscs. jus.gov.on.ca. Information on the Ontario Police College can be found at www.opconline.ca.

Simon Holdoway has studied recruitment issues in police forces in both the U.K. and Toronto, Canada.

The Toronto City Auditor's report on the Toronto police school can be found at www.toronto.ca/auditor.

Quotations on police leadership can be found in Brian A. Grossman, *Police Command: Decisions and Discretion* (Toronto: MacMillan of Canada, 1975).

5. POLICE CULTURE AND ITS IMPACT

Jerome H. Skolnick's quotations are from his *Justice Without Trial: Law Enforcement in Democratic Society* (Toronto: John Wiley, 1976), 44. A similar take on police character is found in the *Oxford Handbook on Policing*, edited by Mike Maguire, Rod Morgan, and Robert Reiner (New York: Oxford University Press, 1994), 1012–13.

The 1969 strike in Montreal is described more fully in Sewell, *Police*, 127.

For examples of police being unwilling to identify fellow officers, see Sewell, *Police*, 183.

For the case of Howard Hyde, see *The Globe and Mail* (Toronto) July 14, 2009, A6.

The best material on police deviance can be found in Chapter 1 of

Clifford Shearing, *Organizational Police Deviance*. The full debate about strip searches can be found in the Bulletins at www.tpac.ca.

6. RACIAL PROFILING

The definition of racial profiling is from David Tanovich, *The Colour of Justice: Policing Race in Canada* (Toronto: Irwin Law, 2006), 18. The judge's quotation is from Frances Henry and Carol Tator, *Racial Profiling in Canada* (Toronto: University of Toronto Press, 2006), 88.

Findings from the Kingston study can be found at http://www.police.kingston.on.ca/Professor%20Wortley%20Report. Kingston.pdf.

The citations of Wortley's studies of Toronto youth are referred to in Tanovich, *The Colour of Justice*, 76–77, and Henry and Tator, *Racial Profiling in Canada*, 50.

The information in the 2002 *Toronto Star* article and the reaction to it is recounted in Tanovich and in Henry and Tator. Julian Fantino's memoir (with Jerry Amernic), *Duty: The Life of a Cop* (Toronto: Key Porter Books, 2009) also includes some of the reaction.

The second series of *Toronto Star* articles were published on February 6, 2010, page IN 1, 4–5, and February 7, 8, and 15. See www.thestar.com/racematters.

The court case from which Justice Harry LaForme is quoted is *R. v. Ferdinand*.

Norm Stamper's book is *Breaking Rank: A Top Cop's Exposé of the Dark Side of American Policing* (New York: Nation Books, 2005). Stonechild's case is recounted in Susanne Reber and Robert Renaud, *Starlight Tour: The Last, Lonely Night of Neil Stonechild* (Toronto: Random House, 2005). The quotations from the Toronto auditor and from Christine Silverberg are from Henry and Tator, *Racial Profiling in Canada*.

7. COMPLAINTS ABOUT THE POLICE

Judge Wood's report is at http://www.pivotlegal.org/pdfs/Report.pdf.

Kennedy's report of RCMP complaints was covered by *The Globe and Mail* (Toronto), August 12, 2009, A13, and an editorial appeared on August 13, 2009.

The police press statement concerning the demonstration has since been removed from the Toronto Police Service website.

The LeSage report is at http://www.attorneygeneral.jus.gov.on.ca. The complaint body established by the provincial government is at www.oiprd.on.ca.

The Special Investigation Unit's website is www.siu.on.ca. The ombudsman's report is at www.ombudsman.on.ca/media/30776/siureporteng.pdf. The 2006 incident was reported by CBC News on February 25, 2010.

8. POLICE GOVERNANCE

The quotations on governance are from Sewell, *Police*, 167–71.

Shearing's comments on the Northern Ireland police may be found in Cooley, *Re-imagining Policing*, 71. The quotation on public and private policing is from *Re-imagining Policing*, 65.

9. POLICE AND TECHNOLOGY

The Ericson quotation about radios is from his *Reproducing Order*, 88-89.

Gladwell's thoughts are found in *Blink*. The quotations are from 225–27.

The details of what happened after the tasering in the Vancouver airport are from an article by Don Rosenbloom and Jim Aldridge in *The Vancouver Sun*, November 27, 2007. The Braidwood inquiry is at www.braidwoodinquiry.ca.

Professor Gartner's critique of the use of video cameras was presented to a meeting of the Toronto Police Services Board on March 30, 2009.

The comment by the chief of police in Victoria about body-worn videos is found in a letter to the editor published in *The Globe and Mail*, February 27, 2010, A24. The Mosquito was reported in *The Globe and*

Mail, March 8, 2010, A13.

The use of halogen lights in helicopters was reported in *The Globe and Mail*, March 8, 2010, A13.

10. ORGANIZED CRIME

An excellent book on organized crime is D.R. Cressey, *Organized Crime and Criminal Organization* (Cambridge, Mass.: Heffer & Sons, 1971).

Criminal Intelligent Service Canada publishes an annual report about organized crime in Canada. See www.cisc.gc.ca.

The data on stolen cars come from a 2003 study by Statistics Canada.

An organized-crime trial that went on for many years is cited in Sewell, *Police*, 73.

For information about organized crime and public infrastructure contracts in Quebec, see *The Globe and Mail*, October 17, 2009, A9.

The preventative role as the most persuasive in tackling gangs is strongly argued in Michael Chettleburgh, *Young Thugs: Inside the Dangerous World of Canadian Street Gangs* (Toronto: Harper Collins, 2007), 162–63.

Regarding IMET and its limitations, see John Gray in *Canadian Business Magazine* (Toronto), September 24, 2007.

The Schertzer story is told in *Toronto Life*, April 2009, by Derek Finkle.

11. COMMUNITY POLICING AND CRIME PREVENTION

The quotation about community policing as a flavour is from Bayley, ed., *What Works in Policing*, 139. The studies that put the positive effects of traditional policing in doubt are found in the same book.

The quotation from the Alberta government is found in Brian Whitelaw and Richard B. Parent, *Community-Based Strategic Policing in Canada* (Toronto: Nelson, 2010), p. 4.

Fantino's quotation is from his book, 299.

Peel Regional Police credit Crime Stoppers with responsibility for five calls a day and seventy arrests made during 2006. Most calls appear to be about drugs. See "Annual Statistical Report 2006," p. 8. The examples of police action to reduce crime, and their effectiveness is from the *Oxford Handbook*, 998–99. An excellent article on the failure of prisons and harsh sentencing is by Michael Jackson and Graham Steward, "Fear Driven Policy," *Literary Review of Canada*, vol. 18, no. 4, May 2010, p. 3.

Information on the effectiveness of social interventions is found in Bruce Kidd and Jim Phillips, eds., *Research on Community Safety* (Toronto: Centre for Criminology, University of Toronto, 2004), p. 135.

Bayley's comments on new policing strategies are found in his *Police for the Future.*

12. OUTLINING AN AGENDA FOR CHANGE

Quotes in support of police actions during the G20 are from an editorial in the *Toronto Star*, July 13, 2010. The report by the Canadian Civil Liberties Association on police behaviour during the G20 leaders' meeting in Toronto in June 2010 is at www.ccla.org.

The final report of the Braidwood inquiry is at www.braidwoodinquiry. ca. A summary of LeSage's comments about police as investigators is found in Chapter 7. Material about failures of the SIU are in Bulletin No. 53, May 2010, at www.tpac.ca.

The placement of Seattle police officers in social agencies is referred to by Stamper, page 107.

Ideas on experimenting with patrol work are found in the final chapter of Bayley's *Police for the Future*. Information on the activities of the Toronto Police Accountability Coalition is at www.tpac.ca.

BIBLIOGRAPHY

Auditor General. City of Toronto. *Follow-up Review on the October 1999 Report Entitled: "Review of the Investigation of Sexual Assaults Toronto Police Service."* http://www.toronto.ca/audit/2004/followupreview_1999_investigation_sexual_assaults_tps.pdf

Bayley, David H., ed. *What Works in Policing.* New York: Oxford University Press, 1998.

——— . *Police for the Future.* New York: Oxford University Press, 1994.

Burbidge, S. "The Governance Deficit: Reflections on the Future of public and Private Policing in Canada." *Canadian Journal of Criminology and Criminal Justice* 47, no. 1 (2005): 63.

Calgary Police Service. Environmental Scan 2007. Calgary. www.calgarypolice.ca/pdf/environmental%20scan%202007.pdf

Cayley, David. *The Expanding Prison: The Crisis in Crime and Punishment and the Search for Alternatives.* Toronto: Anansi, 1998.

Chettleburgh, Michael H. *Young Thugs: Inside the Dangerous World of Canadian Street Gangs.* Toronto: Harper Collins, 2007.

Cooley, Dennis, ed. *Re-imagining Policing in Canada.* Toronto: University of Toronto Press, 2005.

Cressey, D.R. *Organized Crime and Criminal Organization.* Cambridge, Mass: W. Heffer & Sons, 1971.

Cukier, W., T. Quigley, and J. Susla. "Canadian Regulation of Private Security in an International Perspective." *International Journal of the Sociology of Law* 31, no. 3 (2003): 239.

Daly, M., M. Wilson, and S. Vasdev. "Income Inequality and Homicide Rates in Canada and the United States." *Canadian Journal of Criminology* 43, no. 2 (2001): 219.

Davis, K.C. *Discretionary Justice.* Baton Rouge: Louisiana State University, 1969.

Doob, Anthony N., ed. *Thinking about Police Resources.* Toronto: Centre of Criminology, University of Toronto,1993.

Dowler, K., T. Fleming, and S. L. Muzzatti. "Constructing Crime: Media, Crime, and Popular Culture." *Canadian Journal of Criminology and Criminal Justice* 48, no. 6 (2006): 837.

Ericson, Richard V. *Making Crime: A Study of Detective Work.* Toronto: Butterworths, 1981.

——— . *Reproducing Order: A Study of Police Patrol Work.* Toronto: University of Toronto Press, 1982.

Fantino, Julian, with Jerry Amernic. *Duty: The Life of a Cop.* Toronto: Key Porter Books, 2007.

Garland, David. *The Culture of Control,* Toronto: Oxford University Press, 2002.

Gilbert, Richard and Catherine O'Brien. *Child- and Youth-Friendly Land Use and Transportation Planning Guidelines for Manitoba.* Winnipeg: Center for Sustainable Transportation, University of Winnipeg, 2009.

Gladwell, Malcolm. *Blink.* New York: Little Brown, 2005.

Goldstein, Herman. *Policing a Free Society.* Cambridge, Mass.: Ballinger Publishing, 1977.

Grossman, Brian A. *Police Command: Decisions and Discretion.* Toronto: Macmillan, 1975.

Holdaway, Simon. *The British Journal of Criminology* 31, no. 4 (Autumn 1991): 365.

Innes, M. " 'An Iron Fist in an Iron Glove?': The Zero Tolerance Policing Debate." *The Howard Journal of Criminal Justice* 38, no. 4: 397.

Jackson, Michael and Graham Steward. "Fear Driven Policy." *Literary Review of Canada*, vol. 18, no. 4, May, 2010, 3.

Jacobs, Jane. *Death and Life of Great American Cities.* New York: Random House, 1961.

Kidd, Bruce, and Jim Phillips, eds. *Research on Community Safety.* Toronto: Centre for Criminology, University of Toronto, 2004.

LeSage, Justice Patrick J. Report on the Police Complaints System in Ontario. 2006. http://www.attorneygeneral.jus.gov.on.ca/english/about/pubs/LeSage/en-fullreport.pdf

Maguire, Mike, Rod Morgan, and Robert Reiner, eds. *The Oxford Handbook of Criminology.* Oxford: Oxford University Press, 1997.

Newburn, T. "The Commodification of Policing: Security Networks in the Late Modern City." *Urban Studies* 38, nos. 5 and 6: 829.

Newman, Oscar. *Defensible Space.* New York: Macmillan, 1973.

Ouimet, M. "Explaining the American and Canadian Crime 'Drop' in the 1990s." *Canadian Journal of Criminology* 44, no. 1 (2002): 33.

Reber, Susanne and Robert Renaud. *Starlight Tour: The Last, Lonely Night of Neil Stonechild.* Random House Canada, 2005.

Sanders, T. "Rise of the Rent-a-Cop: Private Security in Canada, 1991–2001." *Canadian Journal of Criminology and Criminal Justice* 47, no. 1: 175.

Sewell, John. *Houses and Homes: Housing in Canada.* Toronto: James Lorimer, 1994.

———. *Police: Urban Policing in Canada.* Toronto: James Lorimer, 1985.

Shearing, Clifford. "A New Beginning for Policing." *Journal of Law and Society* 27, no. 3 (2000).

Shearing, Clifford and Jennifer Wood. *Imaging Security.* Cullompton: Willan, 2007.

Shearing, Clifford and Mike Brogden. *Policing for a New South Africa.*

London: Routledge, 1993.

Shearing, Clifford, ed. *Organizational Police Deviance.* Toronto: Butterworths, 1981.

Skolnick, Jerome H. *Justice Without Trial.* Toronto: John Wiley, 1976.

Stamper, Norm. *Breaking Rank.* New York: Nation Books, 2005.

Statistics Canada. Crime Statistics in Canada 2005. http://www.statcan. gc.ca/cgi-bin/af-fdr.cgi?l=eng&loc=http://www.statcan.gc.ca/pub/85-002-x/85-002-x2006004-eng.pdf

Tanovich, David M. *The Colour of Justice: Policing Race in Canada.* Toronto: Irwin Law, 2006.

Tator, Carol and Frances Henry. *Racial Profiling in Canada.* Toronto: University of Toronto Press, 2006.

Toronto Police Service. Environmental Scan. Corporate Communications. Toronto, 2008.

Toronto Star. Articles on racial profiling in 2010. www.thestar.com/racematters

Trojanowicz, R., V. Kappeler, L. Gaines, and A. Normandeau. "Community Policing: A Contemporary Perspective." *Canadian Journal of Criminology* 44, no. 1 (2002): 103.

Valverde, Mariana. "Governing Security, Governing Through Security," in *The Security of Freedom,* edited by Daniels, Macklem, and Roach. Toronto: University of Toronto Press, 2001.

Waller, Irvin. *Less Law, More Order: The Truth about Reducing Crime.* Westport, Conn.: Praeger, 2006.

Whitelaw, Brian and Richard B. Parent. *Community-Based Strategic Policing in Canada.* Toronto: Nelson, 2010.

Wilkinson, Richard and Kate Pickett. *The Spirit Level: Why Greater Equality Makes Societies Stronger.* London: Bloomsbury Press, 2009.

Wilson. James Q. "Thinking about Crime." *Atlantic Monthly* (September 1983): 88.

Wortley, S. and J. Tanner. "Data, Denials, and Confusion: The Racial Profiling Debate in Toronto." *Canadian Journal of Criminology and Criminal Justice* 45, no. 3 (2003): 367.

INDEX